Parenting The Athlete

Parenting the Athlete

By
David Espinoza

E-BookTime, LLC
Montgomery, Alabama

Parenting the Athlete

Copyright © 2017 by David Espinoza

All rights reserved. No part of this book may be reproduced or transmitted in any form or by any means, electronic or mechanical, including photocopying, recording, or by any information storage and retrieval system, without permission in writing from the copyright owner.

Library of Congress Control Number: 2017902464

ISBN: 978-1-60862-681-6

First Edition
Published February 2017
E-BookTime, LLC
6598 Pumpkin Road
Montgomery, AL 36108
www.e-booktime.com

Dedications

To Jake and Matt, my two boys who helped me through rough times. Because of you two I had a purpose in life. To be a responsible parent is not the easiest thing, and at the same time it is the most precious and fulfilling achievement by human kind. Caring for you two with your mom was fun, joyful, and rewarding. When Candi was only 32 years of age we lost her to brain cancer. I was scared, nervous, and anxious. You guys were in grade school – very young. I know you both missed her cheering from the sidelines as I did. As difficult as it was to move on, we did, we survived the storm. What a beautiful thing sports was to us. We overcame with God's guidance. I learned so much as a single parent raising two boys in the world of sports, and it was because of you two that I gained so much knowledge and eventually was inspired to write this book. I truly hope I can help other parents involved in sports. As you both started growing you made me laugh, you made me cry, and you made me become a better father than anyone could ever imagine. I'm proud to be a parent and I'm proud to say that keeping faith throughout all my trials has been an incredible journey. I've been blessed to have had such a miraculous opportunity of parenting such wonderful boys who have made me a very proud dad. One of my many favorite sports' moments with you two has to be the time you played against each other in a college basketball game. This was a total result of hard work and accomplishing objectives. Thank you for always learning and for always being the best kids a parent could ever want.

Acknowledgements

I would like to thank God for all of His guidance throughout this project. I strongly feel that this material will help many parents that have a child involved in sports, whether they are in grade school, middle school, or high school.

Editors: Matt Espinoza, David Espinoza, and Loni Espinoza

Cover Design: Matt Espinoza, Jacob Espinoza

I want to commend and recognize all of the parents or guardians out there that are taking the time to nurture and encourage their children. Support for a child in sports is so important. I know many of you will spend countless hours taking your children to practices or games. The sacrifices you make will all be worth it in the long run.

Contents

Foreword 11

Introduction 13

Why Do Kids Go Out for Sports? 17
Grade School Days Are Crucial 24
Is Your Child Being Coached by the Right Person? 35
When You Don't Agree with the Coach 44
Attending the Games 51
More Than Three Sports in a Year Has Gone Too Far 60
Parents and Referees 67
Talented Child Athletes 73
Can Your Child Play College Sports? 82
Making the Grades is Priority 87
Sports Can Be Very Expensive 94
Don't Be a Parent That Complains to Coaches 100
Good Sportsmanship 107
Conclusion 114

Sources 121

Foreword

by Coach Matt Espinoza

I cannot remember any time in my life where sports were not a big part of our family. We watched and played sports together on a daily basis. It was a natural rhythm of life for us. As my brother and I got older, our experience in sports transformed from recreational to competitive. There were few people more competitive than my dad. He wanted us to be the best we could.

Through the years, there were many failures as well as successes. My dad was always the first one to tell us about either of them. There were times I felt like I could never be good enough, and there were times I thought I was pretty darn good. Sometimes, the hardest part about sports was that my dad was my biggest critic. But he couldn't have been my biggest critic if he had not been my biggest supporter.

There are many different philosophies when it comes to parenting athletes (I'm sure this book will help you develop yours). But I would argue with anyone, that the foundation for successfully parenting athletes is support. That's what my dad did for my brother and I. He supported us any way that he could. He showed up to watch our games, found new opportunities for participation, and helped us develop the fundamentals for the sports we played. As we got into high school and our coaches were responsible for a lot more, he showed his support in different ways. But there was never a doubt that my father cared about us and was willing to help us in any way possible.

He may not be perfect, but he does have years of experience, which includes helping my brother and I use sports to learn life lessons and develop positive relationships. I hope the following pages can help you look at how you are supporting your young athletes and allow you to provide them the best experience possible.

1.

Introduction

I've been involved in the sports world since my grade-school days. My memory is full of thoughts having to do with positive experiences. The elementary school I attended used to be Dimmitt Elementary. It's now called Richardson Elementary School – named after my principal who was there when I attended back in 1971. It's 2016 and I'm fifty-seven years full of wisdom living in Salem, Oregon. I'm writing this book because I want to help every parent or guardian out there. I want to feed you valuable information that will help guide you to a healthier sports adventure.

My parents were not the pressure type as far as sports goes. My dad was always working from labor job to labor job – he really didn't encourage us going out for sports. My mother was a stay-at-home mom. She basically knew nothing about sports, but boy could she cook, keep a house clean, and discipline us kids. There were six kids in our family so as you can see, my parents' priorities were feeding the family and working hard.

Throughout the many years I've been blessed to have experienced so many wonderful things about team sports and individual-type sports. I have witnessed parents and how they treat their kids whether in a good way or a very negative way. I've had a down-hearted feeling watching the children react to the negative. I have experienced winning in a big game and losing in a big game. I have experienced playing injured and not playing because of an injury. I have experienced coaches favoring me and coaches despising me. I have experienced officials picking on me and officials helping me. I wish that I knew back then what I know now.

The most important thing I've experienced is being a parent of two athletes. My two boys grew up with their lives revolving around basketball. I set my mind frame to raise them as basketball players so that one day they could possibly get a college scholarship. This would pay for their education and then maybe later they could possibility play in the NBA. That was my dream for them, not theirs. I'm so lucky that I discovered early on that this should not be about my dreams.

One day, in the late 1990s when my two boys were in middle school, I was reading a pamphlet on parenting. Probably the most important thing that I learned was, *listen to your children*. That's right, by listening to my children it reversed my mindset to start making it about them and what they wanted and not about me and what I wanted for them.

There were times when I wanted to set up a basketball workout for them. They didn't want to work out that day, they wanted to play with some friends. Before my knowledge of good parenting I would make them workout first and then they could play with friends. I started altering my plans to make it about them. They played with their friends first, and then the next day we worked out. My two boys were smiling and full of energy while they worked on their skill sets.

Another example would be allowing your child to follow his or her passion. Later in this book I'll talk more about my older child who had a different passion. He lost the drive for basketball and found an interest in music, he wanted to become a hip-hop artist. It was my job as a parent to listen to him and to support him in what he wanted and not what I wanted.

The sports world has changed so much over the years. Parents have a responsibility in guiding their child athlete to a healthy experience, or at least that's how it should be. With added new sports in schools or club sports outside of schools, the pressures of winning and schedule overload can be a little over-the-top for the young athlete. In this book you will learn many things about parenting your young athlete in a healthy way. You will also be introduced to the dark side of sports which is a little less sophisticated. I'm hoping that this will prevent you from ending up in an uncomfortable situation for the sake of your child.

Of course we all want the best for our children, or at least most of us do. The fact is that parents, for reasons, want to fulfill their dreams through their kids. I'm just as guilty, because it was like that for me while raising my kids during their early days of sports. What a beautiful thing it is when we can actually support them on their gifts and their passion whether it be basketball; music; dancing; debating; swimming; football; track and field; baseball; lacrosse; golf; volleyball; drama; art; band; cheerleading; dance team; robotics; singing; tennis, or soccer.

No, I'm not a sports psychologist, but I have read a book written by a sports psychologist and I've experienced many not-so-good situations. I've also experienced adventures that came out shining like a star.

I hope that this book can give you some ideas that will help you as a parent with your child athlete. Our kids need to learn by example and correct guidance. That guidance is love, support, and good sportsmanship while disciplining them in a positive way.

After you read this book you can collect some ideas that might help you as a parent. I want you to have a wonderful experience while parenting your child athlete whether they are in grade school, high school, or college. There is a way that you can have fun as a family and support your child while he or she is competing in a sport.

2.

Why Do Kids Go Out for Sports?

How did I learn to love sports? It all started when I was watching the varsity football team practice during my recess time when I was in the third grade. I was watching the football team practice while leaning against that tall metal fence. The cage-type fence was designed with many square holes giving me a clear view. There was something about the way the players threw the football and caught it. The excitement of the cheers and getting pumped up was an attention getter. The signals from the quarterback were intriguing. The coaches instructing the team and many more actions manufactured my full focus.

I wanted to be one of those guys wearing uniforms and helmets. They wore purple, silver, and white. The helmets were dark purple with a huge white "D" on the side and the football-practice jerseys were marked up with stains from the dirt and grass. The back of the jerseys had two words written on them, "Dimmitt Bobcats".
So naturally I started playing football with a group of kids at the playground every recess during football season. I could not wait to watch the NFL highlights on Saturdays and then the games on Sundays. This, as a little kid, influenced me to become better at the game.

When football season was over, basketball season would begin and I was that kid that would practice shooting the basketball day and night wherever there was a hoop. My two older brothers played basketball for their school team. I would want to be at every game learning by watching their teams. Their example was a true inspiration that ignited my basketball fever – it became my favorite sport of all time. Watching the high school varsity team on Tuesday and Friday nights was my passion and my number one priority, even if I had to walk by myself to get to the game in the dark and cold weather – I loved watching that much. I still remember the guys I used to watched to learn, Kent Bradford, who stood at 6' 3" and Mark Wohlgemuth at 6' 4". These two guys helped the Bobcats win many games. They advanced to the state tournament and placed second to champions, Hughes Springs in Texas.

To advance to the state tournament in Texas was pretty tough due to the number of districts and regions. Schools would have to first win the district playoffs, then the bi-district playoffs, and finally the regional tournament before advancing to Austin, Texas, home of the state tournament.

When basketball season was over, track and field became the next sport for me. I was intrigued and fascinated by the hurdles and the high jump. It was in the seventh grade that I realized I could become a three-sport athlete, and sure enough, I did. Putting time into practicing the skills needed in both these events paid off big time for me. They each have a certain technique that had to be mastered and it helped me stand out above others because of the time I spent perfecting those skills. While my friends were chasing girls I was perfecting my skill sets in sports.

The number one reason why kids go out for sports has to be, *to have fun*! At least that's how it should be. Okay, so maybe there are more reasons. Before I elaborate on this subject, let's really focus on what we as parents should be sacrificing for our kids. It's not about us, it's about the child and what he or she desires for an interest. It is our job to allow them to enjoy their passion in whatever sport it may be, and remember, don't live your dream through your child, instead, support his or her dream.

There may be times where the parent and child share the same interest. *Following your dad's or mom's footsteps*, We've all heard that expression a few times. It's true, there are so many kids that get inspired by their dad or mom who might have played college ball. They go on to do amazing things in the same sport their parent played.

Another reason kids go out for sports is because the mom or dad want their child to shine in the spotlight – it's exciting to see their child excel and be better than others. The mom or dad also know the techniques for that skill set. The child could possibly be going out for sports because it's a requirement and "no" is not an option. This situation is a storm developing if the child despises the sport. Maybe the child likes golf better than baseball. Dad makes him or her play baseball instead of golf. My personal opinion is that the child will eventually show signs of not having fun at all – it will seem like a job and a fulfillment to honor thy parent. Remember, the number one reason kids go out for sports, is to have fun, not to start working in a job at an early age.

Let's go on to the next reason kids go out for sports. Their friends are playing on the team and they want to be involved to be around their friends. This is a good thing. The social skills come into play. Friends are so important to most children. Despite the fact that they have little interest in the sport itself. They will have fun and they will be introduced to a team environment. Plus he or she will be getting exercise every day. Funny how kids sometimes become outstanding athletes later on due to starting a sport just because their friends were playing. I like this non-pressure situation and how motivated a child can be to learn and be more involved in sports.

Boys and girls also go out for sports because of a high school player or a professional athlete that was seen and followed on TV. For me, that's one of the reasons I went out for sports. This scenario is actually pretty good. Again, there's no pressure added to the child. He or she willingly wants to play a certain sport and improve on the necessary skill set. What's even better is that they are watching an athlete that has mastered the skill set needed to play the game. This is one of many excellent ways to learn and improve – they are engaged and serious about progress in their own mind.

There are athletes out there, believe it or not, that have the talent to be great at a certain sport and yet it was not for him or her. I've heard it over and over for many years. A parent sees a kid that has all the natural talent for a certain sport, but yet because of his or her personality or emotional state, it just isn't meant to be.

Arcie was big, fast, and strong. He made an excellent fullback and linebacker. The only problem is that he did not like to hurt people. In football, hitting is a must and injuries happen. This kid once broke someone's arm in a game. It emotionally drained him. Coaches and friends tried to talk him into staying on the football team. He tried to continue playing but was not happy at all. He finally ended his football career in the early years of high school. Track and field was a much better fit for him – a non-contact sport.

Some kids go out for sports because their parent was a coach and they tagged along to all of the practices watching and learning. To the child it became their environment and if they look up to the coach of the team, well, it's more likely he or she will want to be part of that team some day. I remember having a coach whose kids would always be at the gym shooting baskets on the side goal. All three of them became good basketball players. You could visibly tell that they enjoyed the sport and had fun with the whole adventure.

I'm not saying that a parent should not encourage their child to try a sport. I think that's a great idea. With our two kids we signed them up for soccer, baseball, basketball, or whatever sport they wanted to try. At the end of the season, we asked them if they wanted to continue playing. Baseball, we thought, was much too long and boring. My older son played until the minor little league, and then he decided that basketball was more fun with more constant action. My younger one could not play football or baseball due to a blood condition he had. He did manage to play T-ball one year – the ball was softer. He didn't play minor league. We didn't want him to get hit on the head with a hard baseball. With us it was more of not allowing him to play for medical reasons.

Any way you look at it, we tried to make that decision come from them after they had participated in that sport for one season. Approaching it that way gives the child an opportunity to let you know if it's going to work out for him or her. It's also important to acknowledge what the child's reaction is when you sign him or her up for a sport. You'll get a good feeling by their reaction if it's something you want to carry forward or not.

Before signing up an elementary child for a sport they've never played before, it's a good idea to take them to a few high school or middle school games. Make it a family event, we did that with our kids and we always had fun watching a game while eating popcorn. This visual is so important for the child to get a grasp of the game and to see the way it is played.

Competition is another reason kids go out for sports – it's fun. Being able to compete well with solid skills and determining who the better team is can be a fun experience.

This reason, to me, is probably one of the best. They want to be part of a team and they want to compete against another team.

When I was a child, my family lived in the low-income side of town. We used to play football in an un-maintained pasture. Most of the neighborhood kids would gather and we'd pick teams. Lewis and Fernando were the biggest and toughest among the group. There were no coaches and we didn't want to leave anyone out. So the teams were split up evenly to make it fun for everyone. Lewis would play on one team and Fernando on the other. Why do you think we did it that way? Exactly, because it was more fun making it more competitive. It's no fun when one team clobbers another. Splitting the teams up fairly also gives everyone a chance to participate.

Recognition is another reason that appeals to athletes and sometimes it's mostly the parents that enjoy reading about their child. News is something that's built into sports. And now with social media, athletes' coverage has exploded. I appreciate that since I'm a writer and I do write articles on athletes. I have to admit that being recognized in the newspaper, on TV, or social media platforms has to be uplifting, not just to the athlete, but to the parents as well – it's something an athlete can be proud of when they read their name. In most cases the stories that are covered are about teams or individual athletes that win or maybe accomplish something that people are interested in reading. Losers, not so much, unless a winning streak was broken or they have never won a game. I really think that mindset has to change. Even if you lose the game, you don't lose. Your team has learned and developed in a positive way. If your team improved from last week and worked hard doing the best they could, your team has won already – something to be proud about.

Whatever the reason is that your child began to play sports should not matter. You have introduced your child to something fun and productive. This activity will keep them off the streets and it will initiate exercise to keep their hearts healthy. The important factor to keep in mind is, listening to your child. Are they having fun? Discover what their interest is. I challenge you to adapt and adjust for your child.

3.

Grade School Days Are Crucial

The initial trigger of beginning the sports adventure with your children can be exciting, challenging, nerve-racking, and rewarding. What I wouldn't want to see from any child is the look of disappointment. When that happens then naturally the parents will also be disappointed. Unfortunately many kids end up dropping out of sports before entering middle school or high school.

When my oldest boy was in the second grade I was so excited to see him play in his first game. After handing him a miniature basketball at two years old and following that up with years of teaching him the skill set needed, it naturally brought excitement because I now watched him apply what we had worked on for years. And the best part, I had never seen him as happy as he was that day – full of smiles and energy to get in the game.

It was a little nerve-racking at first because I didn't know what to expect. Would he be able to compete with the other kids? Would he make any baskets? And most important, was he going to have fun? These were thoughts I had going through my head because I wanted him to love basketball and continue it through the rest of his school days. I think many parents feel the same way I did when their child first steps on the court, or field, or whatever sport he or she is playing.

In the first official game that my child ever played in with referees and all, he scored 22 points and finished the game with a triple-double. In the Boys and Girls Club, every kid plays the same amount of time, so he actually played two quarters the entire game. The daily workouts and keeping him going with his younger brother, paid off for him. This was a rewarding experience for my son and for my family.

There are several ways to keep your child smiling, and remember that one of the most important facts of becoming a good parent is to listen. What is it that your child athlete is asking of you? Let's take basketball for example. You have just signed up your child to play for a basketball league. Most youth leagues have volunteer coaches. I don't want to sound like I'm critical of volunteers, because I've volunteered for many years in several areas of sports or at schools.

In some cases the coach is only volunteering because no one else stepped up to the plate. This is a tough situation, because you really shouldn't pull your child out of a basketball little league just because the coach is not really a basketball coach. At this age it's important to teach a child not to quit, ride the year out and commit to the team.

What you do need, is to take action in several ways. I really feel that your child will not learn the fundamental skills the correct way if you don't take action. There is a correct technique on how to shoot, dribble, rebound, pass, and play defense. Basketball also has rules that the coach must know and teach to the kids. The coach can be the nicest guy and a decent human being, but this will not develop your child for the future years. When you don't master a certain skill, the chances of having fun in the future years will fall short.

It's so important to introduce yourself to the coach and ask him or her if they played basketball in high school or college. If the answer is *yes I played in college*, then at least you know the coach must have some kind of solid background knowledge. When practices get going, attend a few sessions and take notes of what the coach is teaching the kids.

Every kid is working hard these days and every year is very important, especially during the grade-school days. And again, this applies to any sport. I challenge you to invest time in your child so he or she can have more fun in the years ahead of his or her athletic adventures.

Johnny was in the second grade when he started playing basketball. He was very tall for his age so the coach put him at the post position. He could rebound the basketball and block shots. The coach never developed him on dribbling the basketball or shooting something other than a layup. Johnny was a star in a grade-school team and his parents were on cloud nine. He continued playing the same position each year – coaches knew him as the rebound and shotblocking superstar. Johnny's parents had all kinds of future ideas and thinking one day he would play Division I Basketball. As the years passed, Johnny continued doing well until his freshman year of high school. All of his peers had grown to be taller than him. He sat the bench the entire year and then during his sophomore year his parents got into an altercation with the coach because of the lack of playing time. Shortly after, Johnny quit the team and never played basketball again. If only Johnny would have learned how to dribble the basketball and also worked on a mid-range jump shot, maybe things might have been different.

Now let's get back to the volunteer coach that never played basketball. And again, this is during your child's grade-school days – more on coaching in a later chapter. The first thing a parent can do is somehow reach out to the community and search for someone that has a passion for basketball. Ask this person if they would be willing to come give a clinic for the team – even if you have to take up a collection and pay him or her. Maybe this person could teach the basic fundamental skills that a player should be learning at the beginner stage – huge in terms of development. Somehow getting connected to someone that has a passion for the sport your child is in will benefit your child in the long run. I'm using basketball as an example but it doesn't really matter what sport.

If you are a parent that has a day job, try to be consistent and put your child at priority, especially in the early grade-school days. The more attention you give your child, the more trust they will have in you. Don't forget about their practices or any kind of forms that have to be filled out. Get your children to the games on time. There's nothing more frustrating to a coach than having players show up late to practices or games. In bigger cities gym space is tight and every minute is valuable. Set a good example for your child, they will learn from watching you.

Stay involved in any kind of team activities, whether it's a trip to the zoo or just an outing at a local park. This is great for team bonding. Players that do things together off the court become better teammates during the season.

I remember the tournament teams my kids played with. Coaches often had activities planned during some of the weekends for the entire team and parents. Whether it was a pizza feed or an outing at the river, it didn't really matter, the point is that the team was together bonding and having fun off the field or court.

I can't stress enough about school work. Keep up with your child in academics. To me grades are more important than sports. I know it might be hard to believe, but there are parents in this world that only care about sports and forget that if a child wants to play in college some day, he or she will have to maintain a 2.0 GPA or better to be eligible. Each college may differ in their requirements, so be sure to do research on this. If the grades come shy of that policy, your child will not play college sports. And trust me, the coaches at the high school and college levels are dead serious about grades. I'll cover academics in more detail in a later chapter.

Leroy was a fast kid, he could break loose and score a touchdown at will during his early years of playing football. His parents were proud of him and talked Division I Football regularly. He did enough to get by in schoolwork and his reading ability was very weak. By the time Leroy reached high school he was leading the league in yards rushed. He was an all-state running back. His senior year there were recruiters coming from everywhere. Leroy's dad was so proud to talk to them. One of the first questions they asked was, "How are his grades?" Leroy could have played at a Division I school, but because his reading level was so low and his grades were skimming by, he eventually went on to play for a junior college – the college was willing to take a chance on him. Had his grades been good, he would have had a full scholarship to play football at a major Division I college. Even playing at a junior college Leroy also had to be aware that if his GPA dropped below 2.0 he would have to pay the scholarship money back and become ineligible to play sports.

The key to helping your child do well in academics, is to continue to remind them how important grades are, not just for sports but for their future careers. Teach your kids how to develop good study habits during their early days of grade school. For some kids it may be easy – they are smart and can retain information better than others. I have to admit that when I was a child I was one of those students that really had to study to do well on tests. I focused on getting my homework done and getting it turned in the next day. Set up a plan for your child to get the homework done before watching TV or playing outside.

Also, I found out that I was more of a visual student. Letters and numbers didn't always make sense to me. When I saw a picture on the bulletin board the whole world changed for me. Discover what works for your child – how can they learn without struggling so much?

Keep up with your kids and know what's going on at school. There's something called "Conference Days". This is where you as a parent have the opportunity to come meet the teacher and find out what your child has been up to. Trust me, this was so helpful to me, especially with my older child who was more social than most. Not so much in grade school, but more in high school. I started working with the teachers so they could help me in keeping up with my child. When he didn't have a school assignment done or missed turning in one, the teachers would email me and I would get after him. It was a great method and it worked for us. My son's grades came up and he started putting in more effort.

It's really important that your child get enough sleep every night. There's definitely a debate on how many hours of sleep a child needs. Talk to your doctor and have him or her recommend how many hours your child should be getting for his or her age.

Staying in shape in the off-season, like summertime, can be a challenge. Running can be helpful if you make it a fun event. There's plenty of fun-run events or walk events going on. This motivates a child to prepare for it. If you are a parent that can participate with your child, that's even better. When my two boys were in grade school we would go out on a jog in the evenings. At first it seemed like a job to them and there were days that they did not like running. They would rather be playing video games or just hanging out with friends. Because I actually jogged with them, they accepted the fact and they found pleasure in the workout. This, my friends, was the way I helped keep them in shape year-round. When they played sports they were not gasping for air like some of the other kids that did nothing during the summer.

During the summers I also took them to Bush's Pasture Park cross country runs. This was an event held on Thursdays in July and I believe they still hold these in Salem, Oregon. They have the one mile, the 3K, and the 5K for different age groups. We ran in those as a family for many years. It was a form of competing with less pressure on winning. It was fun and something that kept all of us in shape. Afterward we always grabbed something to eat on the way home. Anything that encouraged running to keep them in shape and healthy during the off-season was beneficial to their future involvement in sports.

The key is to keep your child engaged in the fun part of sports. Every child is different, maybe your child enjoys camping. Have him or her run the trails or climb a mountain while on a camping trip. The point is that there are so many ways to keep your child breathing by adding cardio to the summer adventure. This is a plus for the upcoming new school year and the sports he or she will be playing. It's much easier to work on the techniques needed for the sport verses getting in shape running during the actual season, and this applies to any age not just elementary age.

Some of the things that might be helpful is to treat your children with something they really love that has nothing to do with exercising. Some kids like watching a movie that is being released in the theaters. Square a deal with them. If they do their running or some kind of cardio that week, then you'll take them to watch a movie. Girls like shopping at the mall, same idea. Kids look forward to these outings and sometimes, to them, it will feel like they've earned this reward.

Your child matters and you are the parent. Teaching them good values can go a long way, not just in the sports world, but in life. One of the most important parts of sports is good sportsmanship. Setting an example for your child at an early age can make him or her an inspiration for other kids. I have to admit that when my kids were growing up I was not a good example at times. I was way too competitive and always wanted them to win and be the best at everything. I had no idea what I was doing or how I was embarrassing them at times. I think the one thing that saved me was my wife and the apologies I addressed at night before they went to bed.

Yelling at your kids when they are doing the best job they can is the worst thing you can do to them. And if tears start running down their face, well, it's time for you to get a hold of yourself and make a change for your children's sake. This is crucial and so important. For me, it was always a challenge controlling myself on yelling at referees for missed calls, or raising my voice when I felt my kids could do better.

It really hit me the day that my second child was in his early grade-school years. His teacher would have all of the students write journals on a regular basis. He brought his folder home one day and I started looking at it. I spotted the journal he wrote and started reading it. I remember the lines that changed the way I raised my kids from that point on. He said, "I really like to play basketball with my family on weekends, but I don't like it when my dad yells at me." After reading what he wrote, and directed straight at me, I started crying. This son and his brother were the most important kids in my life. I was supposed to be taking care of them and loving them. Instead, I was hurting them emotionally and pressuring them to be the best.

That day I was able to get a hold of some reading materials on how to parent a child. One of the most important lessons to me was, *listen to your child*. From that day on I made every effort to listen to my children and to back off of the pressure I was putting them under. There were better ways to help my kids improve their skills. Yelling at them was not going to do the trick. They were going to make mistakes – it was part of learning. Read this carefully, *we have to allow our children to make mistakes*.

I have a great memory of my kids playing basketball in the second and third grade leagues at the Boys and Girls Club. My instructions when coaching them were a little different. I realized that I wanted them to enjoy the experience and to develop their skills while having fun. During some of the games, I pulled my video camera out and recorded the entire game they were playing. I waited to get home before I talked to them about some of the things they could improve on.

I would insert the VHS tape into the recorder and we'd watch the game. I would first point out all of the good things my kids did and I would congratulate them, "Nice job – good move!" And afterward I would kindly point out what they could improve on in a nice soft-spoken voice. That was so effective and positive. This tool of teaching, I feel was one of the best ways I could teach my children because they could actually see what they were doing in a game.

The main reason I recorded those games and some during the regular season was to help them improve on certain skills. If they watched themselves it made more sense to them. With me just talking to them worked a little, but when they actually saw their errors for themselves, it made it a better way to display what they had to improve on.

Also if you use the video for constructive criticism, try to give your son or daughter praise on the good things they did before continuing with the errors they made during the game. An example would be, if they made a bad pass. Clearly the pass was good and a great idea, but perhaps too long of a pass which allowed the defender to pick it and run it back for the score. Maybe ask the child what they could have done differently. Nine out of ten times they know already before you tell them.

Back in those days the camera was a little heavier than in today's world and I didn't have a tripod. I did enjoy those adventures though and don't regret doing that. The sacrifices that we make for our children will pay off in the long run. The next time you see a dad or mom videotaping their child's game, let that be an inspiration for you. Those moments are treasures, especially when you can go back and watch them years later.

There are other ways of course. Sometimes taking your children to a high school game can be fun and rewarding. Pointing out what the players are doing correctly verses the errors they are making can be easier on your child. It's not them you're talking about, and it's a live-visual example while watching the game they love. Buy popcorn or a soda for your child while they watch a game – much more fun and enjoyable to them. Junk food is okay now and then, but not as a habit. Bring one of their friends along to share the experience. And, by all means don't yell at the referees if you disagree with a call they made. Explain to your children that referees are not perfect and that they have a tough job in trying to make the correct call all the time.

It's important to set a good example for your elementary child in any sporting event, whether you're there to watch or participate. I truly feel that it is super healthy for a parent to listen to their child. Find out what it is they enjoy and find out how you can help them grow into a good person. You will be able to tell if your child is having fun or not. It's not easy being a parent. If you become selfless during your parenting years, it will all pay off when your children grow up and become adults, whether they continue to play sports or not.

4.

Is Your Child Being Coached by the Right Person?

Sometimes it's out of our control when our kids get placed with a coach we know nothing about. Many parents assume that just because a coach has the job he must know about teaching the right skills and he must have good communication skills. My suggestion is that you do some research about this coach. Find out everything you can about his or her experience and knowledge of the sport he or she is coaching.

Too often parents find out when it's too late. The child has not learned anything and possibly could end up sitting the bench in the near future – which translates to *no fun*. Maybe your child was not taught the skills on how to hold the bat with the correct stance on home plate. The kids that are playing on the baseball field already knew the skills before playing on the team. As this coach works with the advanced players, your child could possibly have been put aside to watch practices instead of being rotated in the mix of players. And then there's a possibility that maybe the coach is working with your child but not teaching him or her the correct technique. Your child may not be able to catch up to the others in skills.

When you find out more about the coach you'll get an idea if he or she is the right fit for your child. I'm not saying you should pull your child off the team, but what I am saying is that you might want to find someone that can help your child develop the skills needed to get a jump on an early start of skill development.

It's easy for a parent to say, *Oh he didn't get along with the coach so we pulled him off the team.* The problem with pulling a kid off of a team because of the assumption that the coach wasn't a good coach, well, it's a little premature. The first thing I would do is set up a meeting with the coach. Find out why your child isn't getting along with the coach. Ask the coach questions and get solid answers straight from the source. It could be that your child isn't paying attention, or in simple terms, your child is just further behind than the other kids. In some cases the coach will focus on his better players to help the team win games. In the early stages of child skill development every child should be learning equally with the entire team.

After a meeting with the coach you will have a better understanding of his objectives for the team and what he expects from each player. Most coaches will be honest and will respect that you set up a meeting instead of gossiping to other parents. Trust me, I've been around sports long enough to know that parents can stretch rumors while sitting on the bleachers, or by calling their friends.

If for any reason this coach is volunteering and knows nothing about the sport, you have to admire that his or her heart is in the right place. It's not easy coaching, especially if it's a sport you know nothing about. Parents step up to help out at times because no one else will.

In a case where you find out the coach is not a very good coach for teaching skill sets, even though he or she is the nicest person on this planet, don't sit on that situation. Go find someone in your community to help with your child's development. Don't pull your child off the team, this will set an example of quitting when things get rough. Adapt and find a way to finish the season with external help. If you have the money, there are private lessons available everywhere. There are also organizations that provide free skill-set training, free clinics. Look for those opportunities. You can also find a mentor for your child. Lots of college basketball players would help a child.

For parents like me it was easy because I had a passion for basketball and I taught my two boys the skill sets needed. But for a single mom that might not know anything about basketball or for that matter any other sport, it's crucial to get help.

Is there ever a time I would pull my child off the team because of a coach? A coach that I would not want my child playing for is one that is verbally or physically abusive, or in simple words, just not meant to be a coach at all. Or maybe a coach that consistently never shows up on time to practice and the kids are waiting a long time. In those cases, sure you may think about pulling out your child and finding a different team. Those kind of coaches need to not coach sports – especially youth sports. Some coaches will belittle a child for making a mistake during practice in front of the entire team – sometimes to the point that the child will start crying. Some coaches will curse every other sentence to get a message across to the team.

When I played for a high school team, I can count a few times that I was yelled at and put under so much pressure by some coaches. I was a talented field-goal kicker. There was a time when we were playing the number-one-ranked team in the district. Right before halftime we were trailing and we didn't convert on third down. We were within field-goal range and the football was spotted at their thirty-five yard line. I was a young kid playing on the varsity team.

We were trailing, 14 - 16. The coach yelled out, "Espinoza, let's kick it, get out there!" So I hustled out to try and give us a lead going into the half. The center snapped the football to our holder and he quickly placed it on the ground. I made the motion to kick the football, I could see their middle linebacker break through the line and come hard at me – he was very quick. I put my head down and my leg was connecting with the football. As I punched the ball with my foot, the linebacker cracked me on the side forcing the football to swerve slightly to the right and I missed the target by a foot or so. I was on the ground flat on my back and I could hear our head coach yelling at the referees, "That's roughing the kicker – come on ref!"

During halftime, in the locker room, the special team's coach came straight at me with the evilest eyes I had ever seen in him all season long. He was a pretty big guy, maybe 6' 2" 240 lbs. His fast-pace walk and his pointing-the-finger-at-me was something I wouldn't want any kid to face. He stared at me for a few seconds, his face was about one inch from mine. I didn't say one word, but my heart was pounding and I was in alarm mode. I knew I was in trouble and if I tried to explain to this coach what really happened, I was so afraid he was going to slam me against the lockers. He said to me, "Espinoza, there's no excuse for you missing that field goal – an embarrassment to all the team. We should be leading right now." I didn't say one word, and the coach closed his eyes and walked away in disgust. Several of my teammates heard him and also pointed the finger at me.

This coach not only belittled me by not knowing what really happened out there, but he also gave approval for my teammates to hate me and to put the blame on me for not connecting on a forty-five-yard field goal. The head coach knew what had happened – roughing the kicker which the officials missed. I was lucky that the special team's coach *didn't shove me against the locker, it was so important to him that we beat the top team in the district.*

That anger he developed toward a young kid that was still learning and experiencing the game was a good example of a coach that should not be coaching. I'd say that would be a good reason to pull your son or daughter off of that team.

There are coaches that know the skill sets but aren't teaching them during practices, or at least not including your child in part of the development. They focus on their favorite players and the most athletic kids. They want to win games and your child is not part of the plan.

The bottom line is that in order for your child to have fun in sports, he or she will have to learn and master the skill sets needed. In basketball the child needs to master dribbling the ball; shooting with correct form; footing for a defensive stand; passing the ball, and playing defense. Knowing the rules of the game is also important and I've seen many coaches that overlook teaching the needed terms of basketball. What is a baseline on the basketball court? What is the key area on the floor? What is a pivot foot? What is an offensive foul or charging? What is, three seconds in the key?

Let's move on to another scenario. More advanced coaches start developing a fundamental attitude of how a player should play the game. I remember watching the movie *Pistol Pete*. Pete Maravich was a young kid that played with a flashy style. His passes were right on the mark. He played on the varsity team as an eighth grader. When he lit up a no-look pass to his teammate, the basketball hit the receiver on the nose. The coach got angry and pulled Pistol out of the game. The pass was dead on, Pistol had a gift and he went on to play in the ABA and in the NBA. He was a scoring leader and the players were ready for his no-look passes.

Billy's style of playing basketball was flashy and his no-look passes were right on the mark. When he ran the fast break while dribbling he would often pass the basketball behind his back – his accuracy was consistent. The only problem with this is that the coach was set on fundamental play and did not like Billy's flashy style of play. Billy sat the bench and played behind a point guard that played the fundamental style. If Billy was turning the ball over and not collecting assists, I guess I could understand why the coach would bench him. In my opinion, this coach should have recognized Billy's gifts of how he was helping the team. Billy finished the year with his high school team, but the following year he transferred to a different school. He went on to help his new school reach the playoffs – they missed the state tournament by one loss in the playoff. His new team had a winning record and he also packed the gyms with fans that enjoyed his playing style.

    I'm not saying every kid should go out and play with a flashy style. In certain situations, I feel, coaches have to recognize an athlete's unique talent and whether he or she is contributing to the team, flashy style of not.
    I think Billy and his parents did the right thing by finishing out the season, this shows a great example of not quitting on your teammates and honoring what the fundamental coach wanted for his team. Billy went on to do some amazing things with his gift after playing college basketball. In this situation, things worked out for Billy in the long run.
    I want to stress how important it is to have a coach that teaches kids to become decent people. It's a positive notion to encourage good sportsmanship after a game or during a game, by saying "Thank you" to the coaches after a practice – volunteer or paid coaches. In reality, I would rather have a coach that teaches good values to a child and then the basketball skills.

I do want to mention that winning is the goal for any team. Coaches should have that as part of the process. After all it's fun to compete and to achieve as a team. Winning is fun and it's even better to do it as a team. Celebrating after a game is a fun and joyful event. Winning is rewarding and the result of hard work by a team. I don't want to leave an impression that winning is not an important part of sports, because it is and we all know it.

On a side note though, too many coaches are caught up with the winning aspect of sports. It's priority and it's very important to them – we must win! Some coaches will go to the extreme. Example, I was talking to a friend the other day and he mentioned how some coaches were teaching how to grab someone's jersey from behind while playing defense. I actually witnessed a coach telling some of his players, "The Ref won't see you, it's okay." They don't think about what they are teaching the kids. Too many coaches throw their clipboards on the floor when their team isn't executing correctly. Technical after technical throughout the years, when will they learn that it doesn't help the team or the referee's calls the rest of the game? They don't think about the kind of pressure they are putting on the kids, or the bad example they are setting. No coach is perfect, and coaches will lose their cool once in a while, but to repeat the mistakes every year is not acceptable.

I'd rather have my child learning from a coach that compliments the individual's strengths first and how well they are playing in the game, then uses constructive criticism in a calm way. As far as complaining to the referees, I feel a coach has the right to question a bad call that was made, but in a calm way and then accepting what the referee said. Let it go and continue in a positive manner.

A coach that teaches the rules and good sportsmanship is feeding his players good fruits. A team that loses can win if they improve from the last game. Did they cut down on turnovers? Yes they did, okay a big win for the team. Did they improve their free-throw percentage? Yes, okay another win. Winning should not always be about the final numbers on the score board. If that's the only result the coaches want, well, the entire team is headed for disappointment. It's very rare that a team goes undefeated all season long.

Joe was a young kid that was very strong. He was a field event person and won every shot put competition in Junior Olympics. He had not lost one time the entire season. He advanced to the Regional Junior Olympics Track and Field Championships. He did not learn the correct technique because of his strength. He was accustomed to winning and it was important for him to win – that's what he was taught. Well, he got beat by competitors that had mastered the skill to toss a shot put. Joe fell apart and was embarrassed. On his way out of the stadium he was crying and cussing at his parents. He was avoiding the people from his track club that were accustomed to seeing him win. Joe never learned the skill set and his definition of winning was not him improving his technique every week. His definition of winning was the final mark on the shot-put pit. That weekend sports was not fun for Joe, but it should have been. I don't know if Joe had a coach, but if he did, I would not want my child being coached by that person.

I feel that coaches have a responsibility to develop every player on the team. It shouldn't matter if he or she is the last person on the bench. Every child deserves a chance to learn the skills and to be guided toward improvement. Give each kid an opportunity to play during scrimmages at practice. Give them some playing time in a real game – help them improve. I realize that when kids get into high school that playing time will tighten up, because these days in high school, coaches want to play the best players they have to help improve their chances of winning a game. High school summer leagues are different, coaches will play everyone – true development for each player.

In high school, the coach has a different view than the parents. Coaches put the basketball program at top priority, then the team, and finally your child. Parents have the opposite view. They put their child first, then the team, and finally the basketball program. This is true in most cases, but there could be a few parents that might think the same way as the coaches.

5.

When You Don't Agree with the Coach

Not making a team, regardless of what sport, doesn't sit well with the child or the parent. I remember the nerve-racking experience when my two boys tried out for teams. My older boy was tall and more advanced than most of the kids trying out for teams. My younger son was also advanced and seemed to do well among kids his age. As both started growing other kids also began to grow – especially in the tournament teams that traveled.

There was a point in time where the competition was so tough that I prayed and hoped my kids would make their teams. I was fortunate that they both made the team during the grade-school days. My younger son struggled a bit with his height and his speed. He had not matured, fortunately though he could shoot the ball well. Shooting was the skill set he had really practiced on a lot. Coaches paid close attention to that and kept him on the team.

My younger boy did get cut several times from all-star teams that would travel to California for major tournaments. His attitude was so positive because he knew where he stood among the athletes. And, I assured him it was a great experience to attend a tryout that had the top players in the state. It's always a great idea for a parent to praise their child for trying their best at any tryout, whether he or she make the team or not.

During the grade school days there are all kinds of leagues. If your child gets cut from the school team, there are other leagues around. In smaller towns it could be difficult, in a bigger city there are many leagues. The question is, does your child really want to play this sport? If the answer is yes, then find out what skills he or she needs to be working on so that he or she can become a better player. At book signings with my book, *NOZA: A True Basketball Success Story*, I always sign it, "Never give up". It is so important to encourage kids to not give up at something just because they don't succeed the first time.

When your child doesn't make a team and you obviously see the disappointment with maybe some tears running down their face, it's probably not in your best interest to talk to your child at that time. Wait until things calm down a little. Maybe after dinner, sit down and talk to your child. Show him or her that you feel bad and you are very sorry.

Encouragement is a must. What are some of the things that can be worked on to improve? Ask your child that question so that next year they'll have a better chance to make the team. The last thing you want to do is show signs of anger because your child didn't make the team. Competitive parents will have a tendency of showing their disappointment. Believe it or not, I have heard a parent say, "How could you embarrass me like that?" This will only put their child under more pressure, which is not in the child's best interest.

Skill development is so important, it can be the difference between your child and another kid on the team. When anyone puts in the time practicing, it will show on any tryout. I'm not saying this is one hundred percent accurate, because I used to know a kid that was naturally gifted. I never saw him show up at the gym and play with the group.

But when this kid tried out, he was so athletic with natural abilities that he stood out well. There are exceptions, but in most cases, kids that practice their skill set more will have a better opportunity to make the team.

One of the toughest parts of coaching has to be cutting a player from the team. I can't imagine how the coach feels, especially if he or she is a good coach and cares a great deal for every kid on the team. If you are a parent coach, and your child is on the team, I strongly recommend having a one-on-one meeting with the child and then the parents. It's so important to communicate with the child's parents. Explain to them why their child got cut. The reason could be that the skills were lacking, or maybe the child's attitude was bad for the team. Sometimes if a kid never showed up for practices the previous year, coaches remember that and they'll give another kid an opportunity.

Every parent deserves to know why their child didn't make the team. This is more important in grade school and in middle school. In high school things are a little different, but similar. I truly believe that resolution for any kind of questions is better taken care of with a meeting away from the team.

During my *parenting-the-athlete's* days there were many times that I questioned why my kids weren't playing as much as other kids. I'll refer to basketball since that was their sport. This was mostly during their middle school days. Every time I made an assumption I was always wrong, except for maybe once or twice. When I set up a meeting with the coach I always learned a lot about why my kids weren't playing more. I started observing the practices and games and understood what the coach was talking about. It's easy for us as parents to overlook what our children lack in skills. Sometimes we get absorbed in our own child and we become very biased. Throughout the years and to this day I hear parents at the football games or inside the gym make comments that I totally disagree with.

Even parents that have toddlers today can be this category. We want our child to be the best or to be one of the elite players. "Oh my, he is so gifted, everything comes naturally to him," a mom would say. The problem is that she is the only one saying it. "Man, he's a Division I player for sure, can't wait to watch him play for USC," a dad will say. Really, how can anyone possibly predict what a child will be doing past his high school days when he or she is still in grade school or middle school? Once you've met with the coach, you'll have a better understanding.

My eyes were surprised, and I was a very biased parent thinking that my son could play defense. He was great running the floor, dribbling, passing, and shooting the ball. I have to admit that the coach was being honest when he stated that my son did lack in defensive skills.

It was time to get involved, which was really hard for me at the time because I had so much going on with my job and all. I explained, not just to one, but both my kids that I was going to find out why the coach wasn't playing my son more.

I met with the coaches and I asked what would give my child more playing time. The first thing the coach said was, "The defense is very weak and a quick offensive player will blow right by him," the coach responded. I was in disbelief because I thought my son played pretty good defense. The coach encouraged me to watch my son's defense carefully the next game. This was in middle school where he was playing on a tournament-traveling team, just to fill you in on the era.

I decided to challenge the coach and really pay attention to the details of my son's defense and execution. I remember we were playing a very quick team from Portland, Oregon. It's a totally different mindset watching a game and focusing on truth verses, *I don't want to believe what the coach is saying.* My son was playing the wing position defending a really quick guard, and sure enough the opponent just blew by him and scored a lay-up. The coach called a time out and replaced my son with a quicker and better defender. Viewing the game from the coach's perspective really woke me up and I knew I had to do something to help my son get more playing time.

We found a gym we could get into for some work on defensive drills, and if we couldn't get into a gym, we would practice on the sidewalk at home. That's the skill the coaches were mentioning to me. Defense is so important to middle-school coaches and high school coaches, in fact, defense is priority over shooting the basketball to many coaches. If you want your kid to play basketball in high school some day, work on defense drills with him or her. If you don't know anything about defense, well then, find someone in the community to help or hire someone that can teach your child. Make shooting and ball-handling skills a second priority. All skills are important, but defense is one of the most important skills in any game, just my personal opinion – I'm pretty sure many will agree with me.

After a few weeks I noticed my son was getting more playing time. The coach had good knowledge, he had played college ball at the Division I level, this coach knew what he was talking about. He showed the boys several techniques on how to play defense. The combination of me working with my son off the court and the coach on the court, helped improve his defensive skill set. After the next game the coach looked at me and said, "Your son played good defense, did you notice he got more PT tonight?" I answered, "Yes, thank you, he's worked hard."

In most cases, in order for a child to have fun in sports, he or she needs to be participating in the games. There are a few exceptions where the child is having fun on the bench supporting his teammates. If they don't acquire the necessary skill set to contribute as a team member, well, they will be sitting the bench and cheering for the team. When an athlete acquires the needed skills, this is important for the growth of the team. The athlete will challenge his or her teammates in practice.

What about the kids that don't get cut from the team and play very little in games? These kids are amazing and love the sport they are playing in. They enjoy the practices and are always cheering for their team from the bench. I wouldn't say all of them, but some do have huge smiles on their faces and they are happy to be part of a team that travels and plays against other schools. It's not important that they play minutes, and they want to contribute however they can for their team. Sometimes I think these kinds of kids are the ones who motivate the players that do get playing time. Whether in the practice sessions or during an actual game.

I used to think that it must be tough for some of these young athletes, sitting the bench most of the game, but when talking to some of them, I learned different. They are glad to be on a high school team and they are having the time of their lives being part of a team. Most of the high schools around my area have two thousand kids enrolled. It's tough to make the squad. More power to the young boys and girls that are making their sports' adventures a fun experience, because it is a fun and fulfilling experience.

Put your child before yourself. He or she will be the one playing the sport. Make yourself available to attend any kind of team activity that requires parent involvement. Print out a schedule of practices or games so you know exactly when to be there to pick up your child or drop off your child. I was always one of those parents that watched the practices just to see what was going on with my kids. If you are a social parent and have things going on in your individual life, well,

I would like to suggest putting some of those activities on hold while you're raising your kids – this is sacrificing for your child. I'm not saying get rid of all your social events, but try to limit them to allow time for your children – they will remember this for the rest of their lives, trust me.

If your child is showing signs of unhappiness, wait until they are more relaxed and then have a talk with your child. Ask questions in a nice way, try to find out why they are sad or mad after coming home from practice. Ninety-nine percent of the time you'll know by the answers you get and by watching the practices or games. Many times it will be because of the lack of playing time. They have to sit the bench while teammates play a lot more. Maybe they are getting bullied by their teammates or they don't seem to like their coach (we've never heard that one, huh?). Whatever the reason is that your child is not happy, it is your job as a parent to put your selfish ways aside and pay attention to your child athlete.

Don't get discouraged, because one of my sons didn't acquire the complete skill set to contribute until he was a sophomore in high school. He never gave up, and his attitude of working hard, I mean, his intensity and sacrifice to become the best his body would let him, paid off big time. It was so much fun watching him help his teams during his sophomore, junior, and senior years of high school. He went on to play college and minor-league professional basketball. Read *NOZA: A True Basketball Success Story*, you'll learn more about the challenges my son faced and how he overcame.

6.

Attending the Games

One of the many important roles for a parent is to simply attend your child's games. I remember growing up as a kid and how important it was for me to see my parents watching me play in a game. I was one of the athletes that started in a game and played the majority of the time. I'd see how most of my teammates' parents would cheer with excitement for the team. After the game they would take their son and friends out to eat somewhere.

My parents didn't have much money and my dad worked long hours at a minimum-wage job. He supported a large family of six kids. Now that I'm older I understand why they didn't come to my games. There were times where I had to walk to my games and then afterwards I would walk back home – we lived about twelve blocks from the school. There were many times that I lived vicariously through my middle-income or wealthy friends, imagining what that would be like. To celebrate a big victory by going out to eat with my family, what an evening that would have been.

Our role as parents is to support our kids by attending the games. I know that not everyone can afford to do that, but the ones that can, please for your child's sake attend the games. Get involved in your child's life, cheer for the team and your athlete.

Sometimes parents get caught up in their own selfish ways and focus on their hobbies and their own interests. Naturally when their child has a game they won't make an effort to go watch the game. Children are in school only for a few years, those moments are so important for them to have their parents involved in school activities.

I'm so thankful to those parents who drive their son or daughter to regular season games or weekend tournaments. In addition they give rides to several teammates. That is such a positive example to set – helping out your fellow teammates.

When I was a single parent back in the 1990s, my two boys were playing basketball on two different teams for schools and tournament teams. There were times when I needed help. To this day I'm so thankful to the parents and relatives that helped me out. I could not be at both games at the same time, Lord knows I wish I could have. I relied on team parents that I could trust. This was not easy for me because I was overprotective with my two boys.

Most of the time I could be at both their games because they were two grades apart. But during the tournament weekends it was tough. One son had a game in Portland and the other son had a game in Salem. There was no choice for me, I had to ask for help. It was a fun adventure for the son that wasn't with me because he had an opportunity to spend time with a friend and his family – which was a good thing. I can't stress how important it is for parents to get involved with their children's activities. I found myself helping other parents that couldn't be at games. I gladly gave rides to my son's friends – even after practices during high school. It really felt good helping someone out. We need more of this in today's world.

When you attend a game, you not only watch your son or daughter, but you get a sense of the community, plus you become part of a positive scene and can socialize at an event. You acknowledge who your kids are spending time with and you get to know their parents. Sometimes you see old friends that you haven't seen in years. It's just a fun and safe environment for any family.

A child gets encouraged and they feel loved when a parent walks into the gym while they are warming up to play in a game. When your child is wearing a uniform and is part of an actual organized team, there's something about that special moment that only athletes' parents feel. It could be as simple as, *that's my kid*, or it could be that you are so proud that your son or daughter is part of a team and playing in a real game. Maybe you have put in time helping build the skill set needed and you are excited to see the progress in a real game. Not only that, but what a nice break from your daily job. It could make a great stress reliever. Let the stress be in an overtime game, I call that good stress.

One of the things I strongly recommend, as a parent of two athletes and being around sports my entire lifetime, is to cheer for the entire team. Of course you have to cheer for your own son or daughter, but put the team first, make it about each kid on the team.

Speaking from experience, and I'm as guilty as most parents, I used to cheer for my kids at games – didn't cheer for anyone else on the team except maybe a clap or two. I started hearing people say how I bragged a lot on my kids. Well, that didn't leave a very good taste in my mouth – the truth hurts sometimes. I gave it a lot of thought and I started understanding mindfully what they meant. I started observing other parents cheering for just their child. Wow, that put it all into perspective and I started changing my ways. This was a tough challenge for me and with my hard effort at making a strong attempt to change, I came through eventually.

I cheered for each kid when they made a good pass, a steal, or scored a basket. I started putting the team first and I felt humbled and at peace with how I cheered at games.

I once attended a parent night at McNary High School where my two kids ended up playing high school basketball. The meeting was at my older son's parent night. Every year before the season started the coaching staff would host this important meeting to provide valuable information. The head coach said something that made perfect sense, and to this day I remember it.

Head Coach Larry Gahr had much success at McNary High School in Keizer, Oregon. He coached my older son. At the parents night, Larry said that parents normally put their son or daughter at the number one priority, then the team, and then the program. Let's look at the angle from the coaches' view. Coaches put the program at the highest priority, then the team, and then your son or daughter. When parents understand this, they will have a better connection with their child and the coaches. This means that your child may not be one of the starters if he or she isn't contributing to the team. Your child may play less if the opponents are super quick and your child isn't. Your child might have skipped class and therefore will sit the bench if that is the coach's policy. Whatever the reason, be prepared to look at the program first, then the team, and then your child. This is normally what happens during high school.

To be honest with you, I have to admit that when I watched my two boys play on a team, I always wanted our team to win. I was very competitive and there were times where I was very disappointed that we lost the game. If it was an away game, the drive home was very stressful, and all I could think about is, *why did we miss that free throw?* Or, *I can't believe the ref called that with two seconds left!* Am I making a little sense? I wish I would have known all the things that I know now.

I wish I could go back and redo those moments again. I can't, but if you have a child athlete today, please don't have the same attitude that I did back then. Not only will you make yourself ache emotionally, but you will take the fun out of the game that your child just played.

Countless times I apologized to my two boys when I messed up, whether it was during the grade-school days or middle-school days. If I said something to embarrass them, or critiqued them on their play, I always felt bad afterward. Just some advice from someone that's been there, it's so important as parents to apologize to your child for anything that might have impacted them in a negative way. I'm so glad that I learned this lesson by the time they entered high school. I can't tell you how much fun it was for my two boys when their dad spoke of how well they did. Or if the team lost a game, I never got angry, I was very happy that no one got injured and overjoyed that the team played hard the entire game. By high-school age they knew what errors they might have made, they didn't need another person telling them – plus they hear it from the coaches. We did talk about the games, but it was more about what the team could have done to possibly get a victory. We also talked about some of the amazing plays that were made to help the team win. The conversations were more positive and uplifting and we were so excited for the next game.

If your child comes home sad after the game, it's your job and role as parent to encourage him or her. Things are not always going to go the way we want. And a lot of the times it will be because of the message that Larry Gahr shared at the parent night.

When you attend games you can also video your son or daughter. This makes a great memory to look at, especially later in life when your children are all grown up. We all reminisce at some point, and what better way than a fun event with family. I have a memory of when my two boys won their first basketball tournament at the Boys and Girls Club. It was a two-on-two tournament and my second-grade son was competing against third graders. My first-grade son was competing against third graders. I'm so glad I have a video of that tournament, it was all worth it. I like to pull that video out once in a while – such a great memory. I encourage you all to record your child if you get the opportunity. It's so much easier now with today's technology.

Allow your children to make mistakes during the games, it is all part of learning. No one is perfect, not even the best players on the team. Not even the professional athletes. Watch the NBA or the NFL sometime. You'll see mistakes being made all the time. Athletes never stop learning – it's just part of sports. One of the things that drives me crazy watching the NBA is how the players don't use the backboard when they are two feet away. They try to shoot the basketball straight in, and of course it hits the back of the rim and bounces out. I've seen too many last-second shots like that – it costs them the game. In a football game, the receiver doesn't go out of bounds when the clock is running out. In the MLB, a player doesn't put his glove all the way to the bottom and the ball rolls straight under him. I guess what I'm trying to say here is that no matter how great of an athlete one is, they will never be perfect, especially a young kid that's learning the fundamentals of the game. It's okay if your child makes a mistake, that's how they learn.

Once you're at the game, it is so important to conduct yourself well and practice good sportsmanship. This is an ongoing battle in today's sports world, mainly because parents have become very competitive and their focus is always on winning or maybe, *my kid is better than yours.* Too often parents become unbearable to sit next to at a game. Some parents will even make negative comments about another player. I think it's a good idea to think about what you are about to say before you say it. If your comment is negative toward a player or a coach, then don't say anything. More on good sportsmanship in a later chapter.

There are countless times that I've developed great relationships with parents by saying nice things about their son or daughter. It's very easy and I know it will make you feel good afterward. Support each other, it's a long season and we want it to be a fun experience not just for our kids, but for us too. Sports are supposed to be fun, sometimes parents, and I am including myself, start focusing on, *it's all about me and my son or daughter*, and naturally the season will be full of competition among the parents with their own child verses the entire team. Trust me, with that attitude the season will be a long and stressful adventure.

If you are a parent that is experiencing any of this, please take time to change your ways, make it about the team and support each other – it's *our team* not *my team*. There's no "I" in "Team", I like that saying.

Start setting a positive example for your child athlete at games. They work hard at every practice and they do a lot of studying, not just in the classroom, but also learning the plays at practice. Athletes have to do more studying than the average student in school. Coaches are teaching complicated plays on the football field, the basketball court, the baseball field, or the volleyball court – it doesn't matter what sport. The point is that when you attend your child's game, they deserve a positive experience while their mom or dad are watching them execute what they've worked so hard for.

Kevin was a single dad. He had three daughters that were all playing volleyball during junior high and high school. Instead of paying attention to his daughters and their needs for support, he was dating a different lady each month. He was trying to meet someone that could be a mother for his daughters.

This situation caused many problems. His daughters did not want a new mom. Kevin decided to finally listen to his daughters and he stopped dating until his daughters graduated high school. He made a good decision early on when he realized his daughters were struggling with the entire drama. One of his daughters showed signs of her grades dropping significantly.

He changed his ways and started focusing on attending their games and school activities. His daughters became closer to him and it was during his youngest daughter's senior year that they all started encouraging him to start dating again in hopes that he could meet someone. It all worked out in the end because while Kevin was participating in all of his daughters' activities, it was during those moments that he met a wonderful lady. She had so many things in common with him. She also had daughters that played volleyball and sons that played baseball.

Kevin's daughters are very close to him and now that they are all grown up and have families of their own, they visit regularly and stay in touch.

It's not an easy thing to continue listening to your children and raising them the best way possible, but the result is worth it. Children have enough going on in their youthful minds, and to have added stress and worry with what's going on with their parents, well, I think you see my point. I'm not saying that adults have to completely banish all of their activities, but what I'm saying is, focus on your children first, do the best you can to keep them healthy and encouraged.

As a parent, I can't stress enough to pay attention to your child. As adults we have friends that we enjoy socializing with and activities that we enjoy doing. For instance, hanging out with a group of friends from work, or taking a vacation and leaving the kids with relatives. I strongly recommend you put your pleasures and adult activities on hold until your child has matured more and is smiling during challenges of making teams or improving their skill set in any sport they enjoy.

Spend time with your friends when it will not interfere with your child. Maybe alter your vacations to include your kids too. That will bond your family even more. There's going to be so much time for your own vacation when your kids are out of high school and hopefully in college, trust me.

7.

More Than Three Sports in a Year Has Gone Too Far

This subject is definitely open for debate. But if I'd agree with parents that are signing up their kids for more than three sports in a year, we'd both be wrong. Growing up in a small town that only had three sports in a school year was fun and rewarding. In the fall, for girls there was volleyball and for boys there was football.

During the winter, basketball was the sport for boys and girls. In the spring we had track and field. The year was full of games and tournaments and the stadiums were always packed.

That was it, three sports. Baseball was more of a club sport where I came from and usually a summer sport, which would make four sports for some kids. Oh sure, if kids wanted to go golfing, that was a recreational game, like ping pong. There were other games like table soccer (foosball) and billiards. Swimming was a summer activity at the local swimming pool or at the country club. Don't get me wrong, I think more sports are great! Many kids get an opportunity to compete in something they enjoy. Plus some kids may be more talented as far as skills in a different sport. But what is really happening in today's society?

Back then, when the fall sports ended, kids actually received a good break. Their muscles were granted rest, that was what we called recovery time. Anxiety and stress levels came down a bit from the competition and daily craziness.

I'm talking about practices for two hours after school and playing in real games twice a week in basketball or volleyball. Football games were normally once a week because of the pounding the body took and the practices were much longer than basketball or volleyball. In football, players have to put on equipment like knee pads; thigh pads; shoulder pads; hip pads; check helmet chin strap, and adjustments to everything. This takes time before practices and games. After practices and games, same thing except in reverse.

Traveling was part of the whole package. We'd get home late and we were very tired, or should I say, exhausted. We'd get into working on our homework and completing it. Sometimes we'd have to do homework early the next morning.

I have many memories of football seasons beginning with my seventh-grade year. The practices were brutal. The coaches would yell at us for motivation. If we made mistakes, punishments were fulfilled by us running sprints with full gear. Early in September the weather was over one hundred degrees. The practice drills and the memorization of plays were all in addition to schoolwork, house chores, and finding time to sleep. And then when I was promoted to high school everything was much more intense, not only the coaches yelling when we made mistakes, but the practices started with "two-a-days", or in today's world they are called "daily doubles". Why did I play football? My simple answer, the games. I hated the practices, they would drag on forever and sometimes I would block out the coaches' repeated words. A half-hour of standing listening after two hours of hitting, running and executing plays – I just wanted

61

to go home, and I wanted Friday to arrive to have fun playing football in a real game. I knew that the coaches meant well and I knew how important it was to them that we receive instructions on our plays and that we were prepared for a tough opponent. Our young bodies were taking a pounding, not just in practice, but also in the games. At the end of the season, for me anyway, there was always a huge sigh of relief – I knew we were getting a good break before basketball season started, which was my favorite sport.

    What are we doing signing up our kids for more than three sports in a year? Above I was giving you just a brief description of what a season can be like to a kid. I feel that kids look forward to that break from grinding at a sport. And oh my gosh, the multi-sport athletes that are signed up for two sports in one season ... when do they get a break? When do they rest their muscles? Is it healthy when their bodies are not fully developed? When are they getting to bed? Are they being fair to both teams when missing practices or being exhausted? How can they possibly contribute one-hundred percent to either team? With that kind of intense and busy schedule, I'd have to say that dinner is probably at a very late hour every night. These are some questions we as parents have to ask ourselves.

    I remember my two boys playing basketball during the fall and winter. I have to admit that we ate dinner late every night due to practices and games – and this was only one sport. I can't imagine doing two different sports in the same season.

    Don't get me wrong, I do feel that there are a small percentage of kids that can do five sports in a year – and eventually they will risk burnout or injured bodies. The human body can only handle so much. Kids are not machines, and even machines need tune-ups. There are far more kids that can't and shouldn't do two sports in the same season.

It's tough enough just doing three sports in a year. That's what we call, *three-sport athletes*.

    Nicole was in the fourth grade and she had just completed a successful soccer season. She was one of the best players on the team and stood out above the rest. Soccer requires a lot of running during practices and games. Recovery time is crucial to be able to produce the following week. Basketball was the next sport she would be playing. This was her favorite sport – she enjoyed it more than soccer. Nicole was playing in a kids' league that held practices during the week and the games would be played Saturdays with referees and all. This league was so much fun for the kids and they gained great experience.
    An opposing soccer coach had been talking to her mom, Donna, about having Nicole join their upcoming indoor-soccer team. The coach had a daughter that was very talented and he wanted to recruit Nicole to make his team even better. He was aware of her height, speed, and talent. He mentioned to Donna that her daughter wouldn't even have to make it to the practices since she would also be playing basketball at the same time. The coach was insisting and doing anything possible to get Nicole on his team.
    When Donna talked to Nicole about the indoor-soccer team and the coach that wanted her to play on his team, well, naturally to a young kid this sounded exciting and fun. She said yes, she wanted to play indoor soccer as well.
    When the season began it was fun at first, but then the conflicts and tiredness hit home. Two practice schedules, two different game days. It was not only disappointing to Donna, but it was also burnout time for Nicole. She started hating the entire situation. She didn't even know any of the girls on the soccer team. We know how much running there is in a soccer game and then playing in a basketball game?

That took its toll – she was feeling burned out, exhausted, and fatigued.

Not only was Nicole not being fair to her teammates on either team by not playing one hundred percent and by missing practices, but her mom was also driving her to games and practices and dealing with conflicts when game times were the same day. The soccer coach had told Donna that their season was short, but what happened is that they had byes which caused their season to stretch out a lot longer.

The basketball season was going strong and Nicole was fighting to keep up. She was showing up tired to her basketball game after running an entire soccer game earlier the same day. This happened a few times but not all season long – it was a grind. Finally, with one game left in the soccer season, Nicole didn't want to go to the last soccer game. She was not having fun and she realized it was too much for her body and emotional state. Donna encouraged her to tough it out because she had committed to this and should see it through. Donna didn't want to teach her daughter that it was okay to quit.

Nicole was playing in a basketball game with the majority of the season still waiting ahead. At halftime she asked her mom, "Do I really have to go to the soccer game?" After the basketball game, her mom drove her to the last soccer game the same day. She played in the soccer game but was not rested – she did the best she could. After the game she felt so relieved that it was over.

The following year, the coach approached Donna again pleading for her to allow Nicole to play in his indoor-soccer team again. As we can all guess, it was a quick, "No thank you." Nicole had more fun just playing soccer in the fall and basketball in the winter. Her mom was a lot less stressed about getting Nicole's tired body to practices and games.

Sometimes when kids are overworked, and this could be due to multiple sports, they could possibly come down with a stress fracture in the knee, shin, ankle, or foot. I've seen this so many times throughout the years while being involved in sports. Young bodies are still developing and they need the rest.

Playing multiple sports, two practices and two games, can put a kid behind in grades. The tiredness could possibly affect the thinking and listening in class. I'm not saying that this would affect all kids, but I certainly think it would affect the majority.

Coaches of all people should recognize this and not encourage a child to play on their team if that child is already playing another sport that season. Even if it's the same sport but a different team, same situation. If a coach is trying to recruit your child to play on his or her team while your child is playing on another team, please think about your answer, like Donna did the following year.

What else are you leaving time for if your child does multiple sports? You are owned by practices and games and your child is headed to *burnout*. Don't be a parent that wants to prove to the world that your kid can do it, *look at my kid he or she is tough*. The child may be tough but for how long? Some kids end up getting injured or quit because of the grind.

I once read a story in the newspaper about this girl that played volleyball and ran cross country in the same season. This school was a small private school. The article was praising her for doing it all and having fun. The coaches were supportive of this and allowed her to miss volleyball practices if she had a cross country meet. Most of the public schools that I know would have penalized an athlete for missing practice. They could not play in a game, or if they did it would be minimal.

A team is a team and all of the members should abide by the rules. I don't feel special treatment should be given to one player. You win as a team and you lose as a team. You practice as a team and you travel to games as a team. Choosing one sport during that season allows you to be part of a team and gives you the opportunity to put in a one-hundred-percent effort just like the rest of the team members. There's no "I" in "Team".

I don't have the perfect answer to the multiple-sport athlete. I know that sometimes soccer players are used as field-goal kickers in football. Soccer games usually aren't during the same night as football games. I can see how that would possibly work without taking the soccer player away from his or her soccer practice. The football team would only need the player when they practice special teams, and that's usually at the end of practice. It's definitely something doable, but I'm not sure it's the best thing.

Some parents and coaches might disagree with me, but I really feel that we need to go back to the simple ways of when we used to do only three sports in a year. One sport at a time during the season. During the fall, I don't care if it's football, volleyball, cross country, or soccer, just please pick one only. Your child's life will be more productive with less anxiety and stress. And more importantly, their bodies will thank you for it.

8.

Parents and Referees

I'm not going to be the first person to pick up that stone and throw it. I've been around sports for many moons. I was a competitive person in my days, but never thought of the example I was setting to the young kids. Over the years I've learned that some kids don't listen to the lectures we give them. But what does happen, is that they see with their own eyes the example that the adults display during a game. I've heard most of the insults parents have made to referees, "Go back to ref school you idiot!" Who's really the idiot here? "Are you kidding, my grandma can ref better than you!" Really? My grandma could not see very well or walk without assistance. "Come on stripes what game are you watching!" Well, obviously the same game you are.

    Just recently I read about two high school kids spearing a referee from his blindside during a football game. Another incident I've read about was a parent stepping onto the football field and preventing a child from scoring a touchdown. In one basketball game a parent jumped off the bleachers to attack a young kid. This was all due to some bad calls the referees supposedly made. Sometimes winning is so important to the parent that it leads to temper issues and out-of-control situations. If you, as a parent, ever reach this level, please seek counseling because I feel that there are other serious issues in your life.

In my opinion, competitive people that want to win so bad need to draw the line. Maybe what we need to do is start letting the referees do their job. It's tough enough officiating a close game without the fans' distractions. I keep thinking, what it would be like as a software engineer, a job I held for many years before becoming a writer. If someone would have been at my throat constantly – my job would not get done.

We as parents also need to stop living our dreams through our kids. Allow them to discover what they enjoy and support them on it. Help them set objectives to eventually reach a goal in the near future.

I also feel like parents that get involved in sports should make an effort to look at sports in positive ways that are enjoyable, rewarding, and fun, instead of ridiculing the referees. That's why the majority of kids go out for sports ... to have fun! Focus more on the skill-development aspect of your child and discuss the improvements they are making every game. Talk about the great things they did in a game and then bring up the skills they could improve on.

"You forgot to read the rule book you zebra!" Well, zebras don't read books. "How much did they pay you ref – I'll double it!" I'll be the first to admit I wouldn't want to pay a referee double what they make, even if it's the opponent paying him. "Hey ref, did you come from the blind school!" The comments seem to start getting lower every time, I mean really, to include a blind school? In reality the complaints against calls made will not help at all. The only thing it could do is flare up the officials and help your team earn more bad calls. In addition, your child will see your example and possibly fulfill the same thing in the future. One day they'll be doing the same thing to your grandchild.

Being a referee, no matter what sport, is a job. Some do it better than others. There are going to be good calls and inconsistent calls in a game. Our job as parents is not to yell at the officials. Our job should be to behave in a respectful manner. Set a loving example for the people and children watching you.

It's a game, referees will make mistakes. If it was a bad call, then the coach can question the official and the game will continue. It will not help, I repeat myself, it will not help, if we as parents yell at the officials. The only thing that could happen is that the official, depending on his personality, could make it a very long night for you. I guarantee you this will not help your team.

I know that there are officials out there that will pick on a player, simply because they just don't like the way they look. I have experienced this once or twice in my lifetime – it's very rare, but it is real.

I was once playing in a city league game. We had team uniforms, referees, and a few fans up on the bleachers. In our final game of the regular season we were playing a tough team. Our team was well on its way to the championship game the following week. A referee kept calling fouls on me, I was anticipating fouling out before halftime. I kept questioning him, "What did I do?" He never answered, he just gave me dirty looks.

When he called the third foul on me, I pulled myself out of the game – it was a frustrating situation. Everyone on my team could see that I was two feet from the player I was defending. During halftime I walked over to get a drink of water. The referee was talking to one of his friends while I was walking by behind him. He said, "I don't like that guy with the glasses, I don't know what it is about him, but I just don't like him." He turned around as he was saying this and saw me, he continued, "That's right I don't like you."

Naturally I wasn't surprised because that's the impression that I got. I didn't say anything to him, but I knew that I wasn't going to hurt my team's chances of making it to the championship game. I sat out the rest of the game.

A few days after, we set up a meeting with the league's director. My coach, my brother, and myself attended the meeting. The league director was shocked and informed us that he would talk to the official about this. The director also found out that this official was going to be officiating the championship game. It worked out for us because that official did not deny what he said to me and he was not allowed to officiate in the championship game.

At the championship game, I was shocked to see the official there in the stands. I watched him step down and walk over to me. He said, "Hey I'm really sorry about the last game, it was poor judgment on my part, best of luck today." I responded, "Thank you, all forgiven." I tried my best to keep my mouth shut and not say anything that I would regret. My wife and my two little boys were there watching that night.

It's real in today's world, and I do believe that there are referees that are discriminatory, not just in race, but in many other ways. A player could have long hair or a beard, and maybe an official will call against that factor.

The good news is that I really feel that the percentages of bad referees are very low. There are many *great officials* that go through intense training, some even have supervisors that watch them and take notes. They have a stressful job, especially in the playoffs when everyone goes psycho over a missed call. I've seen a lady get so angry when she thought a bad call was made on her daughter, that she actually fell down a couple of rows on the bleachers. It sounded like the official's call threatened her life and she was screaming like an idiot to defend herself.

I have to admit that I have officiated before, just not to the magnitude of a high school game or a college game. It was for a middle-school basketball tournament. It's tough to recall but I think I was getting paid like twenty dollars a game. After I completed my two games, I was so relieved that it was over – it was like a huge weight dropped off my neck and shoulders. If you're an official, I think you get my message loud and clear.

During the games, I had to remember many things, the fouls, and time outs. I had to calm the coaches down when they complained about a call. I had to blow the whistle appropriately, watch the clock, and ignore the abusive language from the crowd. Talking to the players who were not happy with some of my calls was a challenge. And this was all in addition to concentrating on the game on each end of the basketball court. In simple terms, officiating a game is not an easy job.

There's a reason why referees run out of the stadiums, gyms, or fields after the game is over, especially in high school, college, and in the professionals. The crowds are so focused on winning that sometimes our referees are put in a threatening situation.

Through the past years I've heard most of the comments yelled at referees. I'm always surprised when I hear a new one.

I was at an outdoor three-on-three basketball tournament, and I was watching the championship game of a six-foot-and-under division. George was the referee, he was a seventy-four-year-old man that happened to be volunteering that day. This man had been around for years and officiated many high school games in the past.

It was a physical and intense game. A running-clock game with time running out, one of the players drove to the basket and laid up a shot while the defender was playing solid defense. The shot went in – George called a foul on the defender. It was a very hot day – about ninety-five degrees. The players on the defending team complained in anger, but George stood with his call and the score was tied. The offensive player went to the free-throw line and made the shot. The game was over and George was exhausted after refereeing several games that day. Everything seemed to be calming down and the players that lost were walking away – they were holding one of their teammates back, he was furious. All of a sudden this player starts running toward George who wasn't really expecting him. George saw him coming at him, but wasn't really expecting this player to do anything other than yell at him and complain more. The angry player ran straight at George, he used both of his hands to push him on the chest. George fell backwards and landed on his back as his head bounced on hot pavement. George was taken to emergency – he eventually recovered from this incident. He continued to officiate, but now would be only for younger kids.

    We're not perfect, we're only human, so are officials. They do the best they can and we as parents have to respect them and allow them to do their job the best they can. It's important that we try our best to set a good example for our younger generation – Lord knows this world really needs it. Sports seasons are supposed to be fun and exciting. Although we all want to win, the reality is that one team will end up losing after the game is over. If only the kid that pushed George could have had parents that set a good example for him, maybe that incident wouldn't have happened.

    Go out and support your child's grade school, middle school, high school, or college team. Buy refreshments to help the booster clubs. You can't watch a game without food, or at least I can't. And most importantly, be nice to referees and support them, we really need them healthy and energized so they can do a better job making honest calls.

9.

Talented Child Athletes

Have you ever wanted your child to be the best? Have you ever wanted your child to win every competition there is among his or her peers knowing he or she was gifted? Have you ever wanted he or she to make the all-star team and possibly the MVP of the league? I'd have to say that most of us would love that, our child making it to the big times, and to be regularly written about in the newspaper where the entire community recognizes athletes. And then when they get to college some day, more awards and more recognition.

It gets to the point where many parents actually start worshipping an amazing athlete that is so talented. They put this athlete at the highest pedestal – they are totally absorbed with him or her. Kids could be worshipping that athlete too. They want to wear the same clothes, or shoes. They even want to wear their hair like this athlete. And then, maybe at home the parents are even doing everything to meet his or her expectations to keep him or her happy. *Oh yes, my son is the best, no one can stay with him.* Or, *my daughter is so gifted she has natural talent that stands above the rest.* We need to get her the best lessons and she needs to be playing for the best team in the state – the elites.

I encourage you to think about this and what you might be doing to your child. As parents, we need to thing about others on the team, not just our own child. Also, think about what could happen to your child's emotional state when they realize, at some point, that they are no longer valued as a person when they can't produce in sports.

There are two kinds of mindsets, *fixed mindset* and *growth mindset*. In a fixed mindset, a young athlete can have intelligence and skill which can't change too much. Success is a must and failure is not appealing. In a growth mindset, the athlete thrives to challenge himself or herself and failure is a tool used for growth. The young athlete stretches himself or herself to the most they can reach.

I personally like the growth mindset, it's focused on working hard to improving despite any kind of obstacle. If the child loses a game, it is not considered failure, it's considered room to improve and grow.

Pastor Russell had some wise words that really caught my attention and I wanted to share his words with you.

I love sports! There is greatness in the team aspect, self control, training, responsibility, pushing you past your boundaries, and getting a sense of accomplishment. For those things, and the fun of the game, I love sports.

The things that made sports hard for me are, (1) Kids become commodities for adults to live their dreams through or fulfill their own need for success because they view themselves as failures. (2) The winning becomes more important than all the things I mentioned above. (3) The adults rarely present a mature example for the kids to emulate but instead present an immature example.

Also, if you look into the history of sporting events such as the Olympics and Aztecan games, they were usually always for the purpose of bringing the "gods" glory. There is a natural-spiritual combination that occurs within sports that has a lot of connotations on worship ... time, talents, and treasure. Look at how much we pay professional athletes, who our society lifts up to the level of "perfect human being" or saint, and the amount of time that is given over to athletics as a priority over and above things like walking out your faith, spending time with family, caring for others, etc.

My personal history was that in both high school and college, I had scenarios where I went from being an asset on the team to someone riding the bench. In high school, it was because I broke my ankle. In college, it was because I transferred out and then back in. I was horrified and hurt by how quickly people who used to be my biggest fans suddenly could care less about me and what was going on. When you get showered with praise and gifts because of your talent and then, for some reason, that talent goes away quickly or fades with age, you are no longer seen as important, it is a telling thing that shows the heart of athletics in most people's minds.

As you can see, Pastor Russell brings up some solid points. I can see where many parents would put their star-child athlete on a pedestal and worship him or her – a little idol. And like Pastor Russell said, many parents are living their dream through their child. Maybe the parent never made a team in high school, but you can be sure their child will play the sport they loved and you can be sure they will get the playing time that *they never got.*

Let's be parents that get involved in supporting our children in the sport they love, and let's be parents that teach them good values. Think about every member on the team. How can you help the last person on that bench feel like they are just as important as any of the team members? How can you help a player that has ended his or her career because of an injury? How can we make it more about the team and the possibility of supporting each other and having fun while doing that? I really believe that if the parents of a star athlete focus on others, and not just their child's successes, their child will be loved even if something were to happen and they could no longer play sports.

One suggestion I have for parents of talented athletes, is to maybe have them spend time doing other activities with their teammates. Encourage them to take an interest in others. Allow them to build a relationship outside of sports with their friends. Sign them up for a Bible study so they can meet kids in a positive world. Sign them up with a book club or maybe summer camps with their friends. Loving relationships go on forever, even when we're so old that we can't participate in sports anymore.

I don't want to discourage you from helping your own child, because they are part of your immediate family. Working hard to get better is a plus. Setting a goal to some day play in college is great, and if your child is gifted in sports, he or she has a good chance to play college ball some day. Many colleges give athletic scholarships, which means no tuition and sometimes no room and board. This is a great way for them to pay for their college education. My two boys both earned college scholarships through basketball, and had their tuition paid. It's a big relief to the athlete and the parent – college education is so expensive these days.

Talented and gifted athletes play a huge role for their teams. They are the go-to players in a game and they help make other players better. They also represent their school because of the eyes that are on them at every game.

I guess for me, I have learned over the years that when we lost games, whether with my sports career or with my two boys' sports' careers, I would rather see me smiling or my two boys smiling despite a loss. And I would also want them to shake the opponent's hand and congratulate them on a good game played. I encourage you to also try to work at having that mental attitude so that your child can understand that it's okay to lose a game. It's more important to have fun and work hard. It's more important that your child tried very hard and did the best he or she could. If another team executed better and had the better night, then a well-deserved congratulations is imminent for that team.

One of the things that really bothers me right now in professional sports is the simple interviews during post game. To see a talented athlete answer questions on the podium in an unprofessional way, just because their team lost a game, is plain and simple disrespectful. Not only is it bad for the franchise, but also to the opponents who played well and claimed the victory.

I was watching a post-game interview during the NFL football season. The quarterback from the Carolina Panthers would respond in a serious angry way, "Next question" or "We gotta find ways to win, next question". He didn't give any credit to the opponents or he didn't answer the questions in a way that reporters could write something positive and solid. I have to think about how this athlete was groomed growing up and how he was taught that it was really important to win.

Athletes that are at a different level are more respected and looked up to more. They will be talked about in the classroom, the media, with the coaches, and the parents watching games. They will also be talked about by college coaches. Some of our young athletes are already being scouted by major Division I schools. Many are being groomed by certain people because of their talent. *Some day this kid will play in the pros and I want something in return.* At least that's how I feel about recruiters that are scouting younger kids.

Sponsors are out in a hunt for an athlete that will sale sneakers or T-shirts. It's become a money-hungry society. I don't want to get into this area of sports, because I really feel it's another topic. What I do want to suggest, is that we need to pay attention to what we get our children involved in and what kind of people are around them.

One example is the recruiting of child athletes to build a powerhouse team. This is happening in our own cities. Every year I learn that a kid from one high school is transferring to another high school to help that team with a better chance at making it to the state tournament. Because of the talent that your child has, some parents or coaches will go through whatever it takes to make their team a better team. Winning is more important to them than anything else and they'll go through the most extreme measures to get there.

I totally understand if Mom or Dad were offered a new job and it was in a different city. They have to relocate and they enroll the child in the new school. What I don't understand and will not support, is parents that look for jobs in a certain school district just so their child can play on a team. Maybe another player or coach influenced them to join the team so they would become a stronger team. That, to me, is focusing on winning and doing whatever it takes to win. I'm not a big fan of that and I don't encourage it to any parent.

Why? Well for one, it's a disruption from your child's normal environment and friends. Why have your child go through all of the emotional turmoil? Leaving a school that they've been part of all their life is not a healthy situation.

I was that kid years ago. Oh, not for sports reasons, but for other reasons. It was not fun, and I felt like I was in a different world. My friends were gone, I didn't know anyone and I had to start all over. Sometimes a kid could feel that he or she is not accepted in a new school. The team will practice and you will feel a little at home there, but what about the rest of the time? And what about when your son or daughter graduates from high school? They never had the opportunity to establish a good relationship with any student in that short high school career.

Amy was playing in a team that was probably not going to make the playoffs. She had many friends that she grew up with at that school. Amy was a very talented volleyball player. She was tall and she could jump. She was the leader in kills every game.

Her parents wanted her to play on a team that would give her more exposure to college scouts for her future. They had this perception that nothing was going to happen if she remained at the school she was attending.

They reached out to a bigger school in a bigger city. They got to know a coach and they encouraged Amy to play with some of the girls during a summer league. Amy was excited about playing with a better team and making it to the state tournament, with a possible chance to win it all. This sounded pretty good to her and the parents.

So the following year, as a junior, she transferred out of her high school and moved away from her city. Her mom would rent an apartment to establish residency and she would drive Amy to school and then she'd drive to the previous town where she worked. After work she would drive back to the big city to pick up her daughter from her new school. This went on all of her junior year.

When the volleyball season was nearing the end, her team had only lost one game, and they advanced to the playoffs. They made it to the state tournament and they took the first-place trophy. The parents were overjoyed! That's what the whole plan was – even Amy celebrated with her teammates.

Amy was not happy with how the coach used her on the team. He had coached the other girls for a long time and he seemed to put Amy at a second option in many things.

Her senior year it was looking like the team was not going to be as strong as the previous year, but Amy had the green light and was one of the top players on the team.

Amy tried telling her parents that she was not happy and wanted to move back to her hometown – she missed her friends a lot. Her parents ignored all the signs and just wanted what they thought was the best for her. They insisted for her to stay and finish her senior year. In that school she would get all the recognition she would need to play at a Division I school.

Amy was depressed and emotionally confused. She was no longer having fun and really wanted to get back to her friends. Amy was nowhere to be found. The coach contacted her parents and they drove to the school as fast as they could.

A lot of things that went on hurt Amy and she just gave up. She felt that this was the only way her parents would understand that she didn't want to be in a big city away from her friends. She wanted to be with the teammates that she grew up with, and the school that she always loved.

The coach and the parents found Amy behind the school sitting on concrete steps that led to the basement. She was in tears, very depressed and emotionally disturbed.

Her parents immediately pulled her out of the school and enrolled her back at her hometown that she had left.

Amy's senior year was fun. Oh sure, they didn't make the playoffs and their record was not very good. But Amy led in all the major volleyball statistics and she was playing with her best friends and in the community she was raised. Not only that, but she went on to play volleyball at a Division I school, what she always wanted.

Sometimes we have to put our child first and not the dream that we have for them. In Amy's case, sure she was state champion with a team that was put together, but what did it do to her emotionally? I think in her case, she would have been better off staying at her hometown playing with her friends and the community she came from. The friendship ties that will last forever, even after the volleyball days are gone, are priceless.

To love our children is to protect them emotionally and physically. To love our children is to listen to them, I mean really listen to them. Don't make a state championship game more important than the values your child enjoys. In Amy's case she wanted to play volleyball, it was fun for her. She wanted to play a fun game with the girls she grew up with laughing and working hard to become better as a team.

Having a gifted athlete can be challenging. Your child may get to the point where he or she has a *big head,* which means thinking they are superior – better than anyone else. Our job as parents should be to remind them that there is always someone else that's better.

Every year there are kids working harder at their skills. The thing you don't want your child going through is finding out the wrong way. The first time they get beat in a game or a race will be very difficult for them. But, if you inform them that it is okay to lose because there will be times when they face a tougher opponent, it could make a difference in their attitude. Another athlete will be just as good as your child, and that's fine, good friendly competition.

We need to find a way to show our kids that we love them and that it isn't because of sports or their talent, it's because of who they are – their personality and character. Look at it this way, what if there were no sports, what would your child be doing and who would your child be hanging around that would value him or her? That's a good question and something we should all be thinking about.

10.

Can Your Child Play College Sports?

Many athletes in today's world have that drive to improve themselves by working hard and to represent their high school team the best they can. Their vision is to play college ball. They have heard great things from their coaches and from parents that attended the regular-season games and the post-season games.

These athletes are not the go-to players in a game. They are not the standouts for their teams. What these athletes are is part of a foundation that helps a team succeed. They are team players and they are smart. They know their skill-set package well, but they may not be someone that you always read about in the local newspaper.

If you have a child that portrays this kind of character, please encourage him or her. They could possibly get their education paid for through the sport they play. You don't necessarily have to be a player that's being recruited by a Division I school, or a junior college. It just takes perseverance and hard work to follow through and make it happen.

Brandon and Ted played basketball on a team that made it to the state tournament. They placed fourth and only lost one game in a sixteen-team tournament. Ted was one of the players that many junior colleges and Division II schools really wanted. Brandon was not really noticed by any colleges until the state tournament. Brandon was a fundamental player and he stood at 6' 5". The high school team used him to play the post position, but he could really shoot the three-point shot extremely well. Ted could also shoot outside very well and he was also very quick down the court. There were two other guards on the team that could shoot the lights out of the ball as well. This made the team very strong and college scouts were anxious to get some of these players to sign with them.

Ted was one of the players that scouts were talking about. He had it made and he figured the college recruiters were going to come to his doorstep. Don't get me wrong, I really feel that if any athlete is 6' 10" and can play defense and shoot the ball well, I can almost guarantee they'll have a Division I school knocking at their doorstep. Unfortunately, Ted was maybe 5' 10" – there are many athletes with that height as talented as him. Brandon was 6' 5" but didn't touch the basketball as much as the guards on the team.

There were a couple scouts that mentioned to Brandon that they wanted him to play for their university. To be exact, two colleges. Ted on the other hand had several colleges show interest. Ted thought he had it made.

After the state tournament was over, Brandon continued working hard, he wanted to be ready if a college recruiter called him. Ted was not to be seen anywhere for a long time. This was bizarre because previously he would always workout with Brandon, which included pickup games. There was no sign that he had been preparing for college basketball. Ted assumed they were going to come after him, all he had to do was wait around.

Brandon talked to his high school coach about colleges he might be able to play for. His coach gave him a list of community colleges and some of the coaches he might want to call. I can't count the number of community colleges that

83

are out there all over our nation. Brandon got on the phone and started calling college coaches. He was able to schedule days that he could come play for the coaches in an open-gym scrimmage with some of their own college players. The coaches wanted to take a look, they were wanting players that could help their teams. There were three or four schools he was looking at and hoping they would give him a scholarship. Some offered a partial scholarship and some wanted him to walk on – meaning, no scholarship.

Brandon was working hard and doing the best he could for every coach. He finally drove out to the Oregon coast, it was a community college that saw something in him. Something that would help their team. Brandon was the right fit for this coastal community college. The coach called Brandon's dad the following day and wanted to know what they had to do to get him to sign a letter of intent.

After Brandon fulfilled the commitments he had with other college visits, naturally he made the decision to play with the coach that really wanted him. He would get a full-tuition scholarship with meals and a weekend job to pay for his room. Brandon was moved to the three-guard position, which is the shooting-guard position. The college coach was going to use him as a scoring guard focusing on shooting the three-point shot. He had a remarkable two years playing there, and then a Division III school recruited him because of what they saw during his two community-college seasons.

He signed a letter of intent to play at a Division III school and went on to set shooting records for the college. He graduated from college and played two years of minor-league professional basketball.

Ted struggled getting on a team and his basketball career was not as successful as Brandon's career. Hard work pays off if you don't give up. Go after it, there are many colleges that are looking for players to fit their program and to be role players. It's not always about being the star athlete.

And what's more important, you will have fun playing your role in college. You might get your tuition and meals paid for, and possibly your room. Some colleges will even pay for your room, or help you get a job at the college.

Parents, this is something to talk to your young athletes about, because to tell you the truth, I have seen so many kids that have an opportunity to play college sports but yet they don't pursue it for one reason or another. A lot of it is because they don't think they are good enough. They may lose their confidence, or get scared of the big change that might not be as comfortable and easy as high school.

Help your child in any way you can if you see that they do have a passion for the sport they are playing. This will also save you a ton of money. My two boys saved me thousands during their college days because of the sport they were playing. Sure, you will still have to come up with entertainment money for them, or school fees and books. Some colleges won't pay for those, but the good news is, *the savings on tuition and meals.*

I really don't recommend your child get a job while attending college if they are playing a college sport. I'm referring to during the actual season. If they can work it out to have a job during the off season and they can make their studies, I'd say that would be fine. I strongly discourage this during the season.

College practices and meetings are very long. Travel takes up a lot of time during college. There's no time to hold a job during the season. Some athletes have to do their homework at hotels. It's tiring and athletes need their rest – it's very important to get rest.

College sports really work the athlete more than they should. I've seen it, I'm not surprised when I read about the stress fractures or injuries. I respect coaches that give their players time to rest. For this reason I really don't feel that a college athlete should have a job during the season unless it's a must. Some students have no choice, for example if you're a walk-on athlete.

Playing sports in college is definitely an option. It's a tough challenge that takes hard work and commitment in pursuit of landing a spot on the team. Today there are so many different colleges that offer athletic scholarships for a variety of sports making it a possibility for more athletes. Do research, or ask your high school coach to help you out on this. And, whatever you do, make sure that your child athlete truly wants to play sports at the next level past high school.

11.

Making the Grades is Priority

In an earlier chapter I touched on this subject a little bit just to get it in your mind. Let's get into the academics a little deeper. How important are grades for an athlete?

Growing up as a young kid I always wanted to play college football or basketball – some day possibly in the NFL or NBA. Never once through grade school or junior high did I learn that in order to play high school or college sports, you had to have passing grades. The only reason I passed my grades was because I was competing with my fellow students to get a higher grade on tests and homework assignments. It's extremely important that you keep up with your child's academics.

Attend the school conferences, ask the teachers how your son or daughter is doing. You will get the honest answers from the educators of the school. If it wasn't for those conferences I would have never found out that one of my sons was slacking a little, once he got into high school, specifically his sophomore year. He did just enough to be so-called *cool* among his peers.

Today's technology is what I call a friend to parents. Talk to the teacher and if you find out that your child is struggling with grades or just simply doesn't realize how important grades are, it's time to take action. Get the teacher's email address and communicate back and forth. Teachers are willing to help as much as they can. If the teacher doesn't receive an assignment from your child, expect to receive an email as requested. This is such a powerful tool, because your child has no idea that you know what's going on. Once your child discovers what's going on, they'll put in a better effort. They will know you are keeping up with them. That's showing love to your child. He or she may not realize it at the time, but later in life they will appreciate a caring parent. You cared enough to get involved in their academic world.

Grades are a serious element of the sports' world in every way possible. When I was in high school and thinking about college, I asked one of my friends, "What are you going to major in when you get to college?" He responded, "Oh, football – maybe basketball." Some kids really have no clue that grades are important. I went on to explain to my friend, "Football is not a major. I'm speaking of majoring in a certain field, like physical education, psychology, horticulture, math, or science."

A very small percentage of athletes make it to the professional level. The player must pick a field that they enjoy so when graduation comes around they can land a decent job. Even if you're a great athlete, injuries could end your career, and then what?

I'm not going to get into the GPA (Grade Point Average) aspect of it, because I'm sure it varies in some schools. But basically if you can maintain a C average (2.0 GPA) you most likely will be allowed to play sports at most schools. There are exceptions with schools that have stricter requirements than others. If an athlete receives an athletic scholarship from a college, it's important that he or she looks at the agreement carefully. Grades come into the picture – you have to maintain a certain GPA. If the athlete does not comply with the agreement, he or she will be declared ineligible and cannot play until the grades are valid again. Pay attention to this, *some colleges will require the tuition money be paid back.* Before signing to play college sports, read the contract carefully.

I started looking into the importance of grades and sports when Coach Durham, my eighth-grade coach, informed our football and basketball teams about the matter. I realized I had to put in a great effort to keep my grades up.

If your child athlete has no clue about how important grades are, let them know. Coaches at most high schools have programs set up for students that struggle academically. My heart goes out to athletes that have amazing talent but can't make the grades – someone could have helped them. Many talented athletes that could have received a free education through sports failed to get into college because their grades were really bad.

The first thing you want to address to your children is how important grades are. Tell them that if they want to play sports, they must pass their grades. Set up a study time after school every day. No video games or outdoor games until the homework has been completed. Our job as parents is to show love to our kids, help them learn how to study. Even if you have a child that is very bright, without developing good study habits, a struggle is in the horizon during the college days.

In college it's more of a challenge when you're part of a college team. Traveling takes time because of the overnight trips. Team meetings and practices take a lot of time. Your child athlete will have to make a plan and include time management for studies.

Some students have parents that are not educated. They don't know themselves what goes on at school. Some don't even know how to read, how can they possibly keep up with their child? Naturally if people help, they can make a difference in one kid's life. To the people that have helped kids with grades and explained to them the importance, take a bow, you've made a difference. If you see an athlete struggling with his or her grades, try to direct them in the right path. Find help for them. Most schools have some kind of tutoring program, or study table.

Rick was in high school and he was a gifted baseball player. His parents could have cared less about sports and they didn't keep up with anything that went on at the high school.

College coaches from everywhere were trying to recruit him. His baseball career in high school was amazing. He was the best hitter and pitcher on the team. He had the most homeruns in the league his senior year.

Rick got into the habit of copying other people's work and he also cheated on tests from looking over his friend's shoulder. He was a wheeler dealer with some of his teachers, somehow getting them to pass him because he was so talented and popular among his peers.

Coaches from colleges kept calling him to invite him to one of their games. He told all of his friends that he was not going to go to college. Everyone was shocked and they could not understand why he would pass up an opportunity like that. Rick had put himself in a position where he really wanted to play college, but deep inside he knew he would not make the grades. He knew he had cheated himself by cheating the system.

He managed to fake his way through high school and he even graduated with an average report card. He never returned the calls he received from coaches. After a while the college coaches stopped calling him. Rick met a girl during high school and shortly after they were married.

Working minimum-wage jobs and carrying that weight of not playing college baseball, when naturally he had the talent, was very difficult for him. It did something to him emotionally. Sometimes he would take that anger out on his wife or friends.

Even after he got comfortable with his life, he would get embarrassed when he joined in on any conversation. He didn't know anything about the topic because his vocabulary was minimal. He didn't learn much in high school and it was starting to affect him in many ways. He never wanted to be around people that were educated. He only wanted to be around people that were at his level.

If only Rick would have focused on his grades, or if someone would have helped him, things might have turned out differently. This is a sad case, and even though many schools are strict on grades, I'm pretty sure that this is still happening today.

There are kids like Rick that are struggling. It could be that maybe they have dyslexia or something else is going on in their lives. Whatever it is we need to help kids like this so they don't end up like Rick.

Academics, in my opinion, should be the most important aspect while your child is in school. In a majority of cases, an education is what will help your son or daughter land a decent job with an appealing salary.

I played organized sports starting in the fifth grade way back in the 1970s. When I was promoted to high school I could only think about making it to the NFL as a field-goal kicker. Basketball was a long shot since I was only 6' 0" tall and not quick enough to be a point guard. It was kind of strange because I really loved basketball better than football. I had a better chance making it as a professional in football.

My parents were rarely involved in school activities and they themselves were not educated beyond a fifth-grade level. There was no one that could really help me with homework or to encourage me to do well in school. My older brothers helped now and then, but did not advise me that *a good education* was valuable for a future job.

I will give credit to my mom for getting after us when we didn't feel like going to school. She'd come into our bedroom and threaten us with a belt if we didn't wake up and get dressed for school. She would always ask us if we completed our homework. I think what my sweet mom really lacked is informing us why we needed an education. I think deep inside Mom knew she didn't want us to end up like her and Dad, working minimum wage jobs and struggling to pay the rent and feed a big family. Her style of encouraging us to get to school was enough to convince me, I mean that belt in her hand was pretty scary. I don't know about my three brothers and two sisters, but for me, I learned that school was important.

Sure, we all graduated from high school, but only two of the siblings went on to earn a college degree, I was one of them. I'm not trying to boast here and I do believe that probably half of the siblings are living comfortably. What I do want to point out and can't stress enough is, please, for your child's sake, help them understand why academics are so important. Keep preaching it to them all through their grade school, middle school, and high school days.

My older son was a performing hip-hop artist for several years. That was his passion and I supported him on his adventures. To me, it was an extracurricular activity because I knew how tough the music industry was to break into. Don't get me wrong, a lot of people know who "Kid Espi" is and his songs are still being played today. I wasn't going to just let him think that it was okay to bypass an education. I encouraged him to get a college education and to use basketball as his way to pay for it. I wanted him to have a decent job for his future family some day. And, of course it was ultimately his choice to do what he wanted. As his parent, I did my job and gave him options and informed him with valid information. How would his future look? Where would he end up without an education? My poor parents, I used them as an example. I love my parents, they did the best they could and they did sacrifice so much for us kids – truly thankful for them.

Sports should be an extracurricular activity that embodies joy, fun, excitement, and spirit of a team representing the school. For a tiny percentage of athletes, yes, sports will pay for their college education and land them a career in the NFL, NBA, WNBA, PBA, or MLB. And even then, a professional-sport career doesn't last. The lifestyles are very expensive and many will get caught up in a massive debt. Also, players risk a career-ending injury. Don't be that athlete that gets injured and can no long play a profession sport and has no other option. It breaks my heart when I hear a professional athlete say, "What am I going to do now? This is all I know."

If your child gets an education in a certain field, they will have something to fall back on. If they like sports, they can get into a career that fills their passion. There are all sorts, like coaching; sports psychology; trainer; statistician; athletic director; sports medicine; sports writing; broadcasting; equipment design, and many more. Or they could possibly get a career like I did, that has nothing to do with sports. I was a software engineer for thirty-one years. We did talk sports a lot at break times and lunch times.

I can sit here and tell you all the dos and don'ts but it will ultimately be up to you, the parent. It's crucial to guide your son or daughter to have that mental attitude of focusing on grades more than the actual sport they are involved in. I challenge you to put your child first and to help him or her soar through grade school, middle school, high school, and college with passing grades in every school subject. You can do it, I'm rooting for you.

12.

Sports Can Be Very Expensive

Money doesn't grow on trees and there are families that struggle to make ends meet. Many kids have parents that are blessed financially – that's great. But, there are so many kids that just don't have the money to buy basketball shoes; tennis rackets; baseball bats; baseball gloves; shirts; shorts, and many other items. Not just equipment and supplies, but also private instruction, tournament fees, athletic fees, travel expenses, and meals.

There are ways to overcome this problem. When your child is in middle school they are still pretty young and can't really work in the summer. What you can do is help your child find a job that will earn them money. Neighbors might have projects around their house. Mowing the lawn, weeding around the flower beds, or washing their cars. Find work for them so they can earn money and save it for the school season. Start a savings account at the local bank. Teach your child to be responsible financially.

There are options for getting your child signed up for a sport, even if you have no money. Many organizations have scholarships that they offer, look into those. They will pay for your child's athletic fee if your family is low-income. Sometimes if you have more than two kids in sports, the athletic fee will come down a bit making it affordable for a large family.

Fundraisers are always fun. Get a group of people together and have a car wash, a bake sale, or a concert. I remember when my kids were in high school, I actually organized a talent show to raise money for the basketball program. This was very successful, especially the entertainment part of the show, and I'm thinking the head coach used the money to buy warm-up shirts. Another time, my kids were doing Junior Olympics in track and field. We started a bottle drive and raised a lot of money. We actually went from house to house asking people if they had soda cans laying around. You'd be surprised how many people were amazingly generous to support the cause.

It's a matter of just getting it done. You can buy sports equipment for your child no matter what income level you're at, you just have to look for the many options that are out there.

The Gonzales family had six kids and the only source of income was the dad. He worked at a food-processing plant. His pay was below average with no benefits leaving very little money to pay for transportation, the utility bills, and food.

Two of the kids were extremely talented in track and field. They had won competitions at the local level and at the state level in the Junior Olympics. The next level was the regional competition and if they placed first, second, or third, they would advance to the national meet in Florida. The good news is that the Gonzales family had two kids that placed first in all meets including the regional meet.

The bad news is that they did not have the money to travel farther. The family was from the west coast and the travel expense was unattainable. Mrs. Gonzales had a plan that could work. They asked a few friends and family members if they would be willing to help in a car wash on a Saturday. Plenty of locals knew about the talented kids from reading in the newspaper about them.

Mrs. Gonzales went in to talk to the manager at a local grocery store. The manager welcomed her idea and scheduled a Saturday for a car wash. The manager supplied two water hoses and the water. The faucet was off to the side of the store. This was an event that took planning and a lot of help from many people.

Mr. Gonzales found a large piece of white cardboard, and with different color markers he wrote what the car wash was all about including the amount of money they were trying to raise. The poster was colorful and full of meaningful information about the two kids and how they were headed to nationals.

One of the best places for a car wash, in my opinion, is a grocery store next to a busy road. There are so many people that are willing to help kids in a positive adventure, trust me. And also, they can get their car washed for a donation.

The group was ready to go early on a Saturday. If you do schedule a car wash, make sure you are prepared early before anyone arrives to get their car washed. It's important that the water is tested ahead of time, hoses are in place and wash rags with soap in buckets.

When the customers ask about the car wash, be prepared to explain clearly what you're raising money for – people want to know before they donate. Maybe suggest to them that they are welcome to go look at the poster while you wash their car. That's what the Gonzales family did. I've also seen kids hand out a small piece of paper with a clear-written explanation that the customer can read while they are getting their car washed.

Mrs. Gonzales was expecting people to donate a dollar here and a dollar there, maybe five dollars if they were *generous. Even if you get twenty cars at five dollars each, that's one hundred dollars.*

As the car-wash function began, cars started lining up, it was more than they expected and the entire group of about ten people were busy for hours. A gentleman drove up in a brand new Jaguar. All he said was, "Make sure you get the rims." When the family finished washing his car, he rolled down his window and stretched his arm out holding a one-hundred-dollar bill. Mr. Gonzales took a big swallow and smiled saying, "Thank you so much, sir!" The gentleman answered back, "Good luck at nationals."

There were several people from the community that knew about the car wash. They brought their trucks and trailers to get washed. Most of the people were very generous when they saw the kids actually helping out.

The Gonzales family met their goal over and beyond what anyone expected. The car wash helped pay for the plane tickets and hotel bill for their two kids. It took more than just the family to make this event a successful one. It's all about community and helping each other. This was definitely a way that the Gonzales kids could make it to the national meet despite their financial status.

Poverty is unfair, unfortunately it is reality. If there's a will, anyone that really wants to help their children can make that happen. Getting them involved in a sports adventure should be doable, despite the lack of funds. I want to mention that it is also important that the parents not do the fundraising by themselves. Your children need to help and be part of the work it took to raise those funds. It's such a great thing to do as a family. A lesson in learning how to earn your way to a competition can go a long way in life.

I love schools that have booster clubs. These ran-by-parents' clubs help raise money for athletics. Some have even raised enough money to build covered stadiums and all-weather turfs.

When I was in high school back in Dimmitt, Texas, I always wondered who was paying for the football shoes, jerseys, basketball shoes, and meals on away trips. Meals were paid only for the varsity team. Non-varsity teams had to pay for their own meals. Boosters paid for shoes starting in the seventh grade, but not all schools have that luxury. For the schools that have that gift, that's a great thing. And for the schools that don't have that blessing, it is still possible, you just have to step it up and make things happen.

What I wouldn't want to hear from a parent is, "No! You can't play, we can't afford it, you cannot play tennis." A parent that doesn't allow their child to do something productive and positive, is only thinking of themselves and not the child. They are robbing a child from a priceless experience with a group of kids with the same common interest. The money is no object, there is always a way to get funds.

I challenge you to find a way to raise money for your child's sake. Don't let that be an excuse for you to not leave the house. Make an effort, get other people involved in helping you out. There are many people that will help if you ask, but you have to ask. There are many businesses that would help, but you have to ask. There are many coaches that would help, but you have to ask. There are many students that would help, but you have to ask. Are you catching this theme!

With prices rising on athletic merchandise, things can get a little out of hand and all of a sudden your final total at checkout is over three-hundred dollars. Maybe we can put the socks back, we really don't need them.

I would suggest looking at some used sporting goods. There are many stores around that provide those goods. Try Goodwill, one of my second cousins bought some university

T-shirts there for seventy-five percent off. They were in great condition, you'd never know they were used. Shop around, look for sales. Or hit garage sales during the summer – you'll save a lot of money. I have a brother that barters at garage sales all the time. I always hear about what he paid for a tiller or a power saw, or even Nike shoes.

I'll leave you with this, I hope you don't let the price prevent you from signing up your son or daughter for a sport they really love. If your child doesn't get to sign up for the sport they want because of your assumption of no money, what kind of message are you sending your child? Think about this carefully. I'm rooting for you and wishing you the best of luck, never give up.

13.

Don't Be a Parent That Complains to Coaches

Complaints by parents can wear a coach down and make it very uncomfortable for him or her to coach a team.

The common complaint that I've heard from many coaches is *playing time*. That's right, good old PT. Every kid wants to play in the game in front of people – it's fun! Many parents want to watch their child play. Obviously not every kid on the team can be out there at one time. In tennis, there are two players if they're playing doubles. In basketball there are five players out on the basketball court. In football there's eleven players, unless it's Canada then there's twelve players out on the field. Rosters on football teams normally hold about forty to forty-five players.

Parents will begin to complain up in the bleachers, I've heard many in my days. They first start talking to themselves and then it escalates to the person sitting next to them. In a few days some parents will eventually talk to the coach. Their child is not happy on the bench with limited playing time. I have to say that I respect parents that set up a meeting with the coach to ask questions and get answers. See *chapter five* for more on how your child can get more playing time.

Don't be a parent that gossips among the people in the audience. That kind of attitude can only harm your character and embarrass your child. People might feel uncomfortable sitting next to you if that's what they are going to hear. People attend games to watch the team and to root for the team, not to hear some parent complain because their son or daughter isn't playing, you could possibly ruin the entire experience for everyone else.

I've heard parents yell at the coaches from the bleachers, "What are you doing ... he's the best player on the team!" Other parents might think they know a better way to run an offense or defense. You hear all kinds of things in every grade level. Coaches usually know their players well, they see them every day at practice. I'm certain there have been times where a parent knew their child's abilities better than the coach, but I'm sure these are few.

They will yell, "Come on coach, play a zone, man-to-man isn't working!" When a play is designed and the team doesn't execute what the coach instructed, the blame should not be put on the coach. Sometimes players have their own minds or forget the play during an intense game. Parents sometimes assume the coach made that call. It's not always the case, but the assumption is made by the yelling parent from the bleachers. We need to be careful with our complaints about coaches and plays they instruct the team to run in a game.

During the grade-school years, it's not surprising to have parents volunteer to help run the clock or keep statistics on the scorebook. If a coach needs help with important things like keeping statistics or scoreboard, please be the first to help out. It's mind-boggling to see how many parents don't get involved. In most cases one or two parents will end up doing the work the entire season. Every parent should be able to enjoy watching their child. A rotation is much better where you have several parents doing the job throughout the season.

I guess what I'm getting at is the complaint of having to do the clock or statistics. Some parents think because they paid to get into a game they should not have to volunteer at a game – that's extra work for them. Some organizations have to pay the officials, building utilities, use of the facilities, and much more. Some just don't have the funds to hire scorekeepers. I urge you to be a parent that gets involved, it can be a fun experience.

Why does the team have to practice so late? In a large city, gyms, tennis courts and fields are used by many teams. Every team has to be included in the use of the facilities, which could be a swimming pool, gym, or a field. Some teams are lucky and get a decent time and others will just have to live with it. The coaches don't usually have control over that situation. To complain to the coach about practice times is not in anyone's best interest. Sometimes we just have to be thankful that gyms, courts, and fields are available for our kids to practice.

Parents all too often want their child to play a popular position that normally receives more glory than most. For example, in football I'd say positions like the quarterback, running back, or wide receiver get most of the glory when reading the newspaper. You rarely hear about a lineman, which is unfair because they are a big part of why a quarterback or running back are successful. Positions that also deserve credit are the defensive positions. Unfortunately, if you're not throwing, catching, or running with the football, it's very unlikely the fans' eyes will be on you. That's just how it is.

Coaches will get complaints from parents demanding that their child play quarterback, running back, or wide receiver. A mom or dad wants the coach to build the program around their child when it should really be about the program, team, and then their child.

Coaches see players' size, speed, and abilities. Based on those factors, they will place your child at a position that will help the team be successful. During practices if an athlete talks to the coach about a position he would like to try, I'd say in most cases the coach will give him or her a chance.

I think that in the world of sports there will always be players competing for a certain position. It's not up to the parent to decide who prevails and wins the position. It's up to the coaching staff to make that decision. Parents have to understand how it works and then support the team. It's crucial to not complain if your child was not assigned a certain position on the team. What is important is to talk to your child and help him or her understand the reasons why they didn't get the position.

It's also important to encourage your child to work at those skill sets during the off season so maybe the following year they might have a better chance to earn that position. Find that avenue that will help your child in a constructive way, but never complain to a coach that your child should be playing that position.

Norman's dad was a very wealthy farmer. He wanted his son to play on the varsity team and he wanted him to be the kick-off man to start the game and attempt field goals. Norman was an okay kicker but not the caliber that a varsity team would consider.

His dad offered to build a new stadium press box for the football field. The coaches loved that idea and they agreed. During the summer, before the season started, the construction began. Norman was attending daily doubles with the varsity team all summer long.

Norman's dad would talk to the coaches about how his son would love to be on the varsity team, even if he could just kick field goals. The coaches were hesitant to answer his request. They knew he was donating many hours and money to build the press box. All summer long he kept bugging the coaches about his son playing on varsity. It was as if he was already complaining about the coaches not giving him a confirmed "yes" that he would become the starting kicker on varsity.

The summer was over and the press box was complete. It was beautiful and it gave the stadium an uplift. The stairway up to the top of the stadium, behind the stands, was convenient for the announcers and coaches that would be making the calls from above.

When football season started, there was an unknown freshman kid that could really kick the lights out of the football. The coaches had a tryout for the kicker position. Norman was a very popular kid. During practice most of the players watching were rooting for him to get that position. They knew his dad had done all of the work on the press box.

Norman went first, there were about three or four trying out for the kicker spot. They started out with a punt, Norman had a very nice spiral on the ball after the top of his foot connected, but it only went thirty-five yards in the air. The other players followed after him, and their punts were about the same.

Some of the players knew about Joe Vasquez, this kid had real talent and he was about to show it to the coaches. Joe punted the ball sixty yards in the air with serious hang time. There wasn't too much cheering from the players, they could see that Norman was in trouble. The coaches gave every player three punts, and then kickoffs were next, and finally field goal attempts.

The results were the same. Joe easily won the competition, it wasn't even close. The coaches looked at each other and one of them said, "Joe's our man." The head coach agreed with the comment and it was a done deal.

Norman was not happy and his dad was furious about the tryouts. He complained to the coaches for days, but it didn't change the fact that they wanted the best person for the job. It caused a lot of turmoil, because of what he had done for the team and the amount of money he had put into the program.

They compromised by allowing Norman to be on the varsity team as the backup kicker. Norman was going to be on the JV team, but in order for the coaches to keep his dad happy with all that happened, they moved him up to varsity. I can't imagine how Norman felt, because all the players knew why he was on varsity team. It was a long season for Norman and his dad, but they put themselves in that position.

As parents, when we want to do something for the team, we must do it with a good heart intention, and we must do it not expecting anything in return. Make it about giving and not receiving. Don't put yourself in a position like Norman's dad. It only brought an uncomfortable season for his son. Imagine all of the team members knowing this fact during the season. It couldn't have been fun for either child or parent.

Norman could have played on the JV team and gained valuable experience. Instead, he was standing on the sidelines watching the games hoping for his chance to play backup kicker or punter.

Yes, it is your child and you will decide what's best for him or her. It doesn't matter what sport we're talking about, it all applies and comes down to not complaining despite what you've done for the team. The coach is the coach and our job as parents is to understand the school athletic program and the coach's view. And remember one thing, if a team has thirty or forty kids involved and let's say half of the parents complain about something, it can get a bit overwhelming to any coach.

Set a positive example for your children, so when they become parents some day they will remember what they learned from you. I challenge you to not complain to any coach. Instead, let the positive actions do the talking. If your child is the best person for the spot on the team, he or she will most likely be selected.

14.

Good Sportsmanship

We have a responsibility to uphold the best values for our child athlete. One of those values is *good sportsmanship*. While some people may feel that being a good sport is losing a game and congratulating the winners, well, there's actually more to it.

Being a good sport is not only losing with a good attitude, it's also winning with a good attitude. There are players that can really rub it in when they defeat an opponent. They want to embarrass their enemy or yell out not-so-nice phrases. They get that satisfaction of being better than their counterpart. Players realize others are watching them and what better thing to do then to humiliate the team they just beat.

Try to talk to your child about winning and being a good sport. It's perfectly okay for a player to play hard and aggressive with a mindset of winning a game. I definitely encourage that to its full extent. Once the game is over and a victory is claimed, it's time to not only celebrate the victory with your teammates, but also to recognize your opponents' effort. Walk over and shake their hand while mentioning positive words to them.

The other team practiced just as hard all week. They played a tough game and they feel bad enough already for losing. It gives the losing team total respect toward the winning team when the winners acknowledge the losing team's efforts despite the loss.

Let's talk about a losing team being good sports. It's difficult to lose a game, especially if it's a playoff game and the stakes are very high. Players that lose often get angry, not only at their opponents, but at their own teammates as well. They get so angry that they walk straight into the locker room without shaking the opponents' hands. They also start pointing fingers in the locker room, "It's your fault ... you should have caught the ball!"

Talk to your child, help him or her understand that if they did the best they could, they have already won. If they lose, it is commendable when they walk up to the winners and shake their hands, "You played a great game, congratulations." It's that simple.

I do have a suggestion that might help. When your child is feeling down about their loss, talk to them about why they are feeling that way. What was it that caused them to lose the game? And how can they help the team do a better job next time. Another important factor is helping your child understand that the opponent played better that night and they deserved to win the game. In my opinion, accepting that fact can help a child calm down and move on to the next week of practice.

There were many times after games where I always mentioned a few words to my teammates, despite the fact that we won or lost. The words were different depending on the outcome, but they were words of encouragement and compliments. Help your child develop a mental attitude of recognizing teammates' efforts and accomplishments. That helps build great team chemistry and displays good sportsmanship among their own team. And if a teammate struggled during the game and did not perform to his or her potential, it's even more important to speak words of encouragement.

There are many good things to say to a player that made a mistake with seconds left in the game, where his or her team lost in the end.

You didn't lose the game. It was those two turnovers we had in the first quarter and those missed free shots we had in the second quarter. Those three missed lay-ups in the third quarter could have cost us the game. Maybe that technical we received in the third quarter – they scored two points and they got the ball. Your mistake just happened to hit in the fourth quarter and you know everyone was paying close attention. So you see, the entire team lost the game.

It's amazing how good sportsmanship can apply to just about every situation. Even players of the same team can be good sports or bad sports by demonstrating their reactions to their own teammates. We really need to raise our kids to be good sports in any sport they play – it's so important. We all want to win and that's a great goal to have, but the fact is that a competition is about one team winning the game and the other team losing the game.

I like sports that have a tie for an outcome. Soccer can have a tie and football in overtime – a couple of examples. I don't know if you've noticed, but when a game ends in a tie, both teams seemed to be more relaxed when the game was over. If somehow teams could have that attitude, life in sports would be more enjoyable for both sides.

True competitors can display a lack of good sportsmanship to their teammates after a game they just won. This might be caused by the attitude of winning being the most important thing to them, and also perfection being important to them. I'm not talking about kids bragging on themselves, which is all too common, I'm talking about just the opposite. Let's look at Sam's story.

Sam was a kid that practiced every day after school. You could see him shooting baskets on his driveway. You could hear the basketball bouncing a few times on the concrete driveway before he took a shot. The hoop was mounted on the roof with a white half-circle backboard.

Sam was a quiet kid and all action. He was the type of kid that wanted to play the game of basketball error-free. When Sam got into high school the coaches recognized his potential and his intelligence toward the game of basketball. He wasn't super quick, but he was fast enough to be where he needed to be on the court.

This young man learned so much about the game and displayed it so well on the court that the coaches moved him up to the varsity team when he was a sophomore. Sam was a kid that everyone liked, he was very popular and he was respected by all of his teammates, heck, for that matter by most of the student body.

I don't think a competitive athlete would be a normal person if he or she wasn't disappointed when they made a few mistakes during practice or a game. Sam was the type of person that would get down on himself for not being perfect. This focus is not a good thing, and Sam was one of the nicest kids at school and academically he was flawless.

A form of bad sportsmanship can also be displayed by one person that is a perfectionist and did not have a good game despite a big win.

Sam's team was playing their first game of the season against a top-ranked team. The game was intense the entire way through. Sam's team claimed the victory and the fullness of the gym erupted when the last second ticked off the game clock.

After the game, inside the locker room, Sam was sitting on the bench looking down sadly. Some of the dads were coming inside to congratulate the team. Sam was not happy because of two turnovers he had the entire game. Those *turnovers resulted in two baskets for the opponents. That's all he could think about. He blocked out his thirty points including twelve for twelve at the free-throw stripe, his eight assists, his five steals, and his ten rebounds.*

One parent expressed, "Good game Sam, you were amazing tonight!" Sam responded as he looked sad and disappointed, "Yeah, yeah, sure." It was like the world had ended for him and he had nothing else to live for.

Being a good sport, believe it or not, is also your attitude displayed among your teammates. You can be a kid like Sam and still need improvement on good sportsmanship.

Parents can sometimes be the worst display of good sportsmanship. Imagine what kind of example you are setting for your child. Their eyes see this and guess what they will do when they become parents? I wouldn't say all of them because some kids see the bad example and they themselves don't want to be like that. Sometimes the reverse effect takes place, but I'd say the higher percentage will follow the parent's lead.

As I was writing this book, I took a break the other night and watched one of our local high schools play their season opener at home. The officials were doing the best they could, and sure, they missed a few calls. And then the game was closer and another inconsistent call was made.

A few parents stood up and yelled some not-so-nice things to the referee. There was a gentleman that stood up right behind me. He yelled at the top of his lungs, "You are terrible, you want my glasses!" Naturally I had to turn around to see who it was. He already looked stressed. He was about fifty or so years old. Whatever his reasons were for yelling continuously, it was definitely not the place to display bad sportsmanship. I really felt like saying something to him, but I refrained since it was a parent of one of the players I knew. I think if he would have continued yelling, the crowd monitor would have walked up and said something to him.

Parents sometimes will point out a certain athlete from the opponents. For some reason this player did something like throw an elbow at one of their team players. The rest of the night they will continue to crucify this kid that was already penalized for the infraction.

Sometimes it's best to just let the officials handle the technical fouls and then leave it behind. These kids are all learning and don't deserve to be embarrassed. Some kids can handle that kind of criticism better than others. Some kids get hurt emotionally when they hear the fans yelling things at them in an isolated situation. Fans need to be good sports about handling something they don't agree with. It's okay to not agree with something a player did that was a violation, but it's not okay to point him or her out and continue the badgering the rest of the game.

We're not perfect, and I'm not going to say I myself have never displayed bad sportsmanship, because to be honest with you, I have to work at it each game. What I can tell you is that each game has gotten better over the years. When my wife attends games with me I'll often ask her, "If I ever yell at an official for a bad call, would you give me a little elbow on the side and remind me?" She always laughs at me when I say, "I'm not saying anything to the refs this game." I think the more we practice at being good sports the better we will get. For me it has improved tremendously over the years – it feels great.

Sports are supposed to be fun for everyone. And games are supposed to be great entertainment with crowds that have the same common interest as we do. Games have rules and players are penalized when they break those rules. The officials are not perfect, and if we were to do their job we'd find out that we aren't perfect either. Think about what kind of example you are showing your kids. Good sportsmanship is crucial and must be practiced at every event. This prevents any kind of negative escalation at any game, but it only works for parents putting in a good effort to model this for our children.

15.

Conclusion

I still remember when my kids shined as athletes. Those moments will always be planted in my head. Those are great memories to have, and for me anyway, I really enjoy reminiscing about those days. The time they won their first two-on-two tournament. Or the time they hit clutch shots at the buzzer to win a game. Or maybe the time they played college basketball against each other.

My two boys, Jake and Matt, played at the highest stage in their college leagues. They helped their teams make it to either the state championships in high school, or their college championship tournaments in post season. I couldn't have been more proud of the experience they had with their teams throughout the years. You see, I witnessed them playing their unselfish role as team players. I really feel that team communication and collaboration was one of the reasons their teams were so successful in high school. All of the teammates followed the coach's instructions and all of the teammates worked hard at their game, even during the off-season.

No one really knows what I went through as a parent of these two athletes. I can't count the number of games I sat and watched these two play. I can't count the number of practices I attended, parent meetings, fundraisers, doctor appointments, and supervising parties with their friends.

I can't count the number of times I prayed for their safety during a game or just for them making it through school another day and surviving any bad influences. The sport they played was a true blessing for our family to be involved in, especially because they attended a public school that had over two thousand students. Nothing against a public school, but most are more diverse than a private school.

My personal opinion, and you might have a different one, is that when your child makes it to the high school team, please do the best you can to just be a support system for the program, the team, and your child – in that order. Let the coach be the coach, let the officials make the calls, and allow your child athlete to make mistakes. I know that for some of us parents it's more difficult because we think we know better than the program or the coach, but in reality we probably don't. Oh and about allowing your child to make a mistake? Yes, it's important to talk about improvements in skill sets, but first always talk about the great things they did at practice or in games. Talk about the academics as well, how are they doing in school, and then suggest some constructive criticism in a positive way.

High school kids are learning and it's important to guide them, maybe explain to them why it isn't a good idea to stay up past midnight, or maybe what could happen if they continue to hang around groups of people that are headed in a wrong path. I think most of you parents out there understand my view.

Here's some words of wisdom that I definitely recommend. Get involved in your child's academic world. Attend the school conferences and find out what subjects they are struggling with – it will pay off later. Email is a powerful tool for you to keep up with your child's assignments and whether they are being turned in. I never had a teacher refuse to send me an email to inform me that my son did not turn in a paper. In a majority of cases, your child will start doing better.

I want to be honest with you about nutrition. I was a single parent at one point while raising my two boys. During the middle school and high school days it was just us three. I'm so embarrassed to tell you that I was not a good role model when it came to nutrition. Hamburgers, pizza, and soda were cheap and fast. I'm guilty as charged for being a bad example in healthy eating. Believe it or not I still struggle with my diet, but it's getting better.

It was my younger son, Matt, who showed me how healthy eating was a true benefit in the sports world. He started drinking water instead of soda his sophomore year and eliminated all the junk food. I'm not the nutrition expert, but I do want to recommend that you encourage your child to start eating healthier. I saw the amazing results when my son stuck to a diet, not only did he lose extra weight, but he gained plenty of muscle and he grew about seven inches from his sophomore year to his senior year.

Let's leave you with some tips about sleep. The REM (Rapid Eye Movement) is so important. It is the sleep stage when the body is maximizing rest. Find out from your doctor how many hours of sleep your child should be getting at his or her age. Rest is a must for a child athlete. With practices and late homework nights, their bodies need to get that rest.

A difficult situation for a parent is the one where their child does not want to play sports or a certain sport. Jake, my older son, enjoyed the game of basketball for many years. As he grew older, I learned that he was playing basketball just to keep me happy. His real passion was music, he wanted to become a recording artist. He displayed that so well right in front of me and I was too blind to see it.

The world changed with our father-son relationship when I accepted the fact that I had to support him in his passion, not mine. If you take anything from this book that I have written with my whole heart, take this, get to know who your child is and understand what he or she is asking. I mean, really listen to your child. If it's music, dancing, mechanics, or fishing they enjoy and have a passion for, support them in that adventure. Don't be a parent that makes them continue playing a sport that is making them unhappy.

And I really don't mean during their elementary years. I think it's great to introduce all kinds of sports to them. When they reach an age which they themselves can determine whether it's right for them or not, then it's time to listen well and support them in what they want.

Injuries are real and happen often in sports. I encourage you to always know if an injury is bothering your child. I'm not referring to soreness of the muscles, I'm referring to limping or constant aching of a certain body area. Whatever the case may be, please treat the injury and have your child stay away from activity until it heals. You need to immediately see the doctor and follow his or her orders.

I remember once, my younger son, Matt, had sprained his ankle pretty severely during a 2002 summer-league game. Unfortunately, there was only two weeks before he was supposed to start practicing with an all-star team called, Oregon Ice. This was the first year that he made that team. He was so excited and did not want to miss that trip to Nevada where his team would play in the Adidas Big Time Tournament. I wish I could take that moment back. He did not want me to take him to the doctor to check it out. I felt really bad for him. I do believe that this is the time where you should not listen to your child. I listened to my child, but with that in mind, I made him stay off that ankle for a solid week. That was hard for him, if you knew my child you would agree. He slowly started walking on it after a week, and then slowly started shooting baskets. In a few more days he started testing his cuts toward the hoop. I know he was doing this in pain, but he wanted to be ready for that big tournament. Again I asked, "Are you sure you don't want to go to the doctor to check it out?" He responded, "No Dad, if I do they won't let me play in the tournament."

To make a long story short, he did very well in the tournament with an ankle taped up securely and ice after every game. When we returned from the tournament, he gave his ankle time to heal more. Then days later the basketball season was getting started his senior year. I took him in to get an athletic physical. The doctor said, "Mr. Espinoza, your son fractured his ankle awhile back and he still has a little swelling. You're lucky it healed right."

I encourage you to take your child in to the doctor no matter what he or she says. Matt was lucky like the doctor said. I would not want your child to have a fractured bone and then it not heal correctly.

Keep in mind that there is a dark side to sports. Try to steer your child away from any of those sides. Steroid use to gain strength not only does damage to a child's health, but it is also illegal and could end your child's career in sports. Cheating by not being honest about your child's age just so he or she helps a team win is very wrong. The dark side of sports can also be coaches that are abusing young athletes. Kids being starved, for example in wrestling. They need to lose weight to make that division of a lighter weight. Runners can get dehydrated by not keeping enough fluids in their bodies. There was once a girl that developed anorexia – an eating disorder. She ran many miles a day without eating much. These are just a few examples you should really pay attention to if your child is showing any of these signs. Be involved and be aware at all times.

Sports can be a wonderful experience for our young children, not only during the grade-school days, but also in high school and in college. They learn so much by being part of a team. They have an identity that entertains crowds and it gives them pleasure hanging out in a positive environment. Athletes make parents proud and they also set work-ethic examples to other kids that watch them. Teammates gain social skills and team-building concepts. They learn how to lose as a team and they learn how to win as a team. Playbooks are studied and plays are executed well with given practice and progression. Athletes do better in the classroom because of the exercise they are getting consistently every day. Some athletes earn college scholarships – free tuition and sometimes room and board. Families spend time together when they travel to watch their child play in a tournament – priceless. Athletes stay in good shape physically and they feel good about themselves. Sports can be used to thrive for progress using failure to grow, not only as an individual, but as a team as well. Athletes can stretch their abilities beyond measure.

I'm sure there are more benefits when your child plays sports. One of the most positive has to be the friendships they make while playing on a team. They get to know the other kids, especially when they travel together on away games. They get to help each other, not just on the field or court, but off the field or court as well.

I hope that I have given you some helpful tips and I hope that you will take advantage of what I have learned over the years. I've been around the sports environment for a long time. As I'm writing this book I'm nearing fifty-eight years old, or should I say fifty-eight years wiser? I've seen many things and I've learned from my own mistakes. I don't want you to get caught up in some of the mistakes that parents are making in today's world of sports.

Your children deserve to have a fun, positive, and educational experience in the world of sports. I challenge you to love your children by supporting and guiding him or her in training hard, in playing hard, and in developing an amazing good-sport ethic.

Remember, the number one reason kids go out for sports is too have fun! Make that a priority. I'll leave you with one final thought. Value your child the same while he or she is playing sports and in the same way if they were not playing sports. Value his or her teammates the same while playing sports and when they are not playing sports. Show love to everyone on the team and everyone that attends the games. And yes, even the officials.

Sources

All of the material that I've written is based on my fifty-plus years of experiences in the world of sports. In each chapter I have written, short, true stories that were transferred from my implanted memory. These stories are written in italics. The names of these true people have been fictionalized to honor their anonymous status.

I am a parent, early in life my wife and I were raising two little boys in the world of sports. In 1994 I lost my wife to brain cancer, she was only thirty-two years old. I became a single parent that continued raising two boys in the world of sports. I learned so many lessons, some that will benefit you. What I've written is to help you and your children have fun in the world of sports.

Other Books by David Espinoza You Might Enjoy

NOZA: A True Basketball Success Story

*The Professor Grayson Boucher
Plus More NW Sports Stories*

Poor Kid, Wealthy Kid

Poor Kid, Wealthy Kid II

Books can be ordered at **DavidEspi.com** if you want them autographed. They are also available to order at Amazon or any retail book store.